£1.65

THE TOPICAL TIMES

FOOTBALL BOOK

D.C. Thomson & Co., Ltd.
London — Manchester
Glasgow — Dundee

To: MAGNUS
FROM GRAN & GRANDAD
MERRY XMAS
1981

CONTENTS

ALLAN EVANS
Aston Villa

STEVE FOSTER
Brighton

7

DALG

— "FOUR TIMES BETTER THAN KEEGAN"

says Danny McGrain

What makes Kenny Dalglish a football superstar? Opponents, team-mates and managers give their own personal view of the Liverpool and Scotland striker

DANNY McGRAIN *(Celtic)*

"I'm totally biased about Kenny. We joined Celtic on the same day and practically grew up together. But I'm still certain he is the best player in Britain.

"He is four times better than Kevin Keegan will ever be. He's a better finisher. If my team were awarded a penalty in the last minute of a vital game, I know which player I'd bet on having the cool head to do the job properly.

"It's about all-round ability when you compare the two. Kenny could be asked to play sweeper or full-back one day, and he'd do well. Could Kevin?

"Can Kenny get better yet? If you ask me he has been at his peak for the past eight years!"

PAUL HART *(Leeds United)*

"Kenny always seems to be a quiet, reserved fellow off the field, doesn't he?

"But during a game he does his share of shouting and bawling at team-mates if he thinks they are not pulling their weight.

"That's to say nothing of the verbal stick he can give opponents. I once knocked him over with a bad foul and he was up on his feet in a flash calling me a big, lanky English so-and-so.

"That was the end of it, though. Kenny didn't come looking for revenge.

"Many folk think Kenny is the finest off-the-cuff player around, believing his attacking style is purely instinctive. I disagree.

"Kenny is brilliant, but I'm convinced he thinks very deeply about his game. How else could he keep one step ahead of defenders and be so cool, calm and clinical?"

PAUL HART

JOCK STEIN
(Ex-Celtic manager, now Scotland boss)

"Kenny's attitude is perfect. He's always supremely fit, anxious to play and eager to do well.

"He's not judged on the same level as any other player. The fans expect much more from him than from others. Unless his performance is stunningly brilliant, he is classed as having a bad game.

"Just being terrific isn't enough when your name is Kenny Dalglish.

"He has a scoring record which averages out at a goal every two games for club and country. That speaks for itself.

"Folk say he doesn't play as well for Scotland as he does for Liverpool. That's eyewash. He may have his off-days but they are just as likely to happen in a club game as in an international.

"His attitude to Scotland matches is exactly the same as it is for Liverpool — absolutely right."

8

JEFF WEALANDS
(Birmingham City)

"The goal Kenny hit past me in one of my first games in Division One illustrated the difference between him and run-of-the-mill strikers.

"He hit a volley from 18 yards. I'm sure 90 per cent. of players would have chested the ball down first.

"That would have given me time to narrow the angle. But Kenny just spun on the spot and smashed the ball out of my reach. I was helpless.

"Dalglish is on a different wavelength to other strikers. A goalie really has to sharpen his thinking to read Kenny's intentions."

JEFF WEALANDS

PHIL THOMPSON
(Liverpool team-mate)

"Kenny fancies himself as a bit of a joker. We sit and listen intently to what he is saying, trying to follow the story. Then Kenny starts rolling around in hysterics at the brilliance of his wit. And we haven't even realised he's cracked the punch-line!

"He's a great Billy Connolly fan, too. He once let us hear one of the Big Yin's tapes. Kenny couldn't stop laughing while the rest of us hadn't even come close to understanding the joke.

"However, although he may be strictly Fourth Division when it comes to the funnies, as a player he is in a different league.

"And since he joined Liverpool from Celtic in 1977, I'm convinced he has become an even better player."

BOB PAISLEY (Liverpool manager)

"Often you buy ability and just hope the player's character holds up. When we signed Kenny we knew all about his ability.

"But if Jock Stein had told me Kenny would prove such a model professional I mightn't have believed him. If I'd been told exactly how good a trainer and timekeeper he is, I would have been scared off. Too good to be true!

"Kenny has the first requirement of any successful pro — he detests losing. He also feels he's entitled to dole out advice on the field and voice his opinion, even when his own game falls below standard.

"Not that that happens very often.

"He has something of Bill Shankly in him. Shanks' motto was 'Concentrate on the simple things. Do them well and success will follow.' That's Kenny's motto, too."

BOB PAISLEY

ALLY BRAZIL
Ipswich Town

STEVE
PERRYMAN
Spurs

STEVE
COPPELL
Manchester
United

TWO STAR STEVES

11

SEMI-FINAL "BLACK-OUT" I'LL NEVER FORGET!

Spurs goal-ace STEVE ARCHIBALD tells why.

WHAT a first season I had in English football! 20 goals in the First Division for Spurs, a place in Jock Stein's Scottish international squad, a 'two-leg F.A. Cup Final at Wembley, plus a cup medal. It'll be hard to beat that in future.

I have a stack of marvellous memories from the last year. But the incident that still stands out in my mind is the one that I can't really remember at all! That was in the F.A. Cup semi-final against Wolves at Hillsborough.

Thirty seconds left on the clock, and a place at Wembley seemingly booked with a 2-1 lead.

Then came the most shattering blow I have ever experienced—the incredible penalty decision given against Glenn Hoddle by referee Clive Thomas.

Once Wolves had equalised I went into a kind of trance. My mind went blank. I was playing from memory, I can remember nothing about the first period of extra time.

When the whistle blew for half-time I thought there must have been a mistake. It seemed to me we had only played about two minutes.

Looking back I believe we were lucky to get away with it at Hillsborough. A better team than Wolves would have seen us off in extra time. We just weren't 'with-it' at all.

But having survived that set-back there was no way we were going to let them off the hook a second time, and in the replay my goal-scoring pal Garth Crooks put us 2-0 up, and Ricky Villa finished them off.

Obviously the Wembley finals must rank as one of the highlights of my career—but no greater than winning the Scottish League with Aberdeen, or for that matter actually signing for Spurs.

When I talked to manager Keith Burkinshaw for the first time he told me of the superb new stand that was going to be built, of the players he had and the players he wanted. It was clear that Spurs and I had the same views. We both wanted the very best.

Last season was the first step towards achieving it—and I believe the side can only get better.

People talked a lot about my partnership with Garth Crooks. Between us we scored over 40 goals last season. But that understanding didn't come overnight. You have to work over a period, and the longer you play together, the better it becomes.

I must admit I was amazed to finish up last season as the top scorer in the English First Division. I never dreamed I would be in that position. Everything went far better than I hoped.

The thing was I found it much easier to score goals in England than I had done in Scotland.

It's a different game altogether. The play in Scotland is much tighter and much tougher. It's far harder to find goalscoring chances in the Scottish League.

I think it's due to the Premier League system. With only ten clubs involved you can be up with the leaders one week and fighting relegation the next. Everyone is looking over their shoulder all the time—and that doesn't help anybody relax and play football.

Most teams are more concerned with defence than attack. In the English League many more teams are trying to play open football.

There's also the referee's approach. In Scotland the tackle from behind has not yet been outlawed. Defenders go straight through you when going for the ball.

It's far different in England. Tackling from behind is penalised, and so defenders hang back and jockey you, trying to nick the ball off your toe when they can.

I found it took me a while to adjust to the different style.

Being able to settle in the south was my only worry when Spurs came for me. Several Scottish strikers with big reputations have gone to England and failed to do themselves justice.

I never had any doubts about my ability to make the grade

footballwise in London. But setting down off the field is a different matter.

In the event I had nothing to worry about. My wife Maureen and I found a home in the countryside away from the big city, and we love it.

I feel far more settled at Tottenham than I did at Aberdeen. Financially I am more secure. It may be easy to say that money is not everything, but it certainly seems important when you haven't got any!

Quite apart from the money, joining Spurs has helped me establish myself in the Scottish squad, and that is very important to me.

In recent seasons I have become known as purely a goal-scorer—and I certainly do enjoy putting the ball in the net. I'm never completely satisfied with a game if I haven't scored a goal,

even if we have won the match.

But I wasn't always a striker. When I joined Aberdeen from Clyde I was basically a mid-field player, and at Clyde I must have played in just about every position on the field.

I'll never forget the day I played in goal at Hampden Park. The Clyde 'keeper was injured in the first half and I took over in goal. The first time I touched the ball was to pick it out of the net! But somehow we hung on and won the match 5-3.

Billy McNeill, now manager of Celtic, was the man who took me into the big time. He was manager at Clyde for a spell, and after he went to manage Aberdeen Billy signed me for the Dons. Then he converted me from mid-field into a striker—and I haven't really looked back since.

We had a good side at

Aberdeen. We kept getting close to winning honours—beaten finalists in the Scottish Cup once and runners-up in the Premier Division once, plus two losing League Cup finals.

In my last season it looked like we would miss out once again when we lost in the League Cup final, and in the semi-final of the Scottish Cup. Nearing the end of the season we were trailing Celtic by eight points in the League.

But we put everything we had into the last few months, winning ten and drawing five of our last 15 games, beating Celtic twice to pip them for the championship.

It was a good time for me to leave Aberdeen—as a winner.

My first season came to a climax at Wembley Stadium. I hope every year at White Hart Lane will be as exciting.

CYRILLE REGIS
West Bromwich Albion

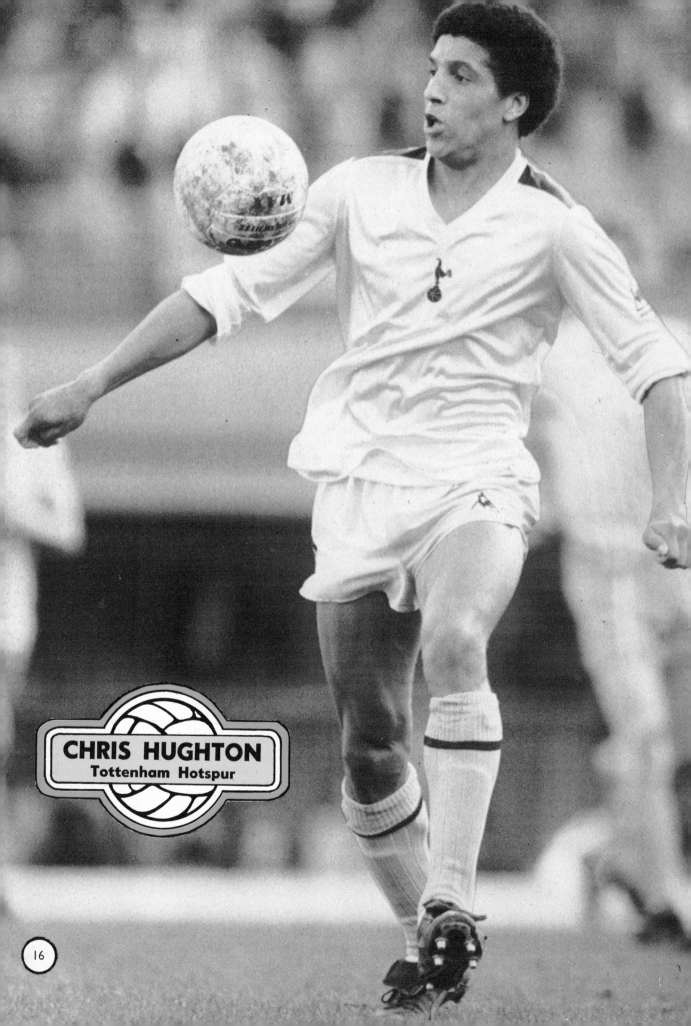

CHRIS HUGHTON
Tottenham Hotspur

16

GERRY DALY
Coventry City

17

IT'S CRAZY.
BUT I LOVE IT

PETAR BOROTA (Chelsea) talks frankly about football in Britain

I HAVE spent two years in English football playing for Chelsea. I've enjoyed it, but still I think to myself— 'the English—they're mad!'

Football in England is very different from the game in my country of Yugoslavia. For example the number of matches.

You cannot expect to do well in competitions like the World Cup or the European Championships when your players have so many games.

Players with the top teams can play 60 or 70 matches a season. And then without a break they go off to play for England. I think it's crazy!

No other country in the world demands so much from players. Top footballers have to play two matches in one week and sometimes three.

I watched England in the last European Championships in Italy. After a long home season there was no doubt that several of them had lost their edge.

Before the World Cup finals next year the teams taking part will all have at least two months to prepare—and England must learn this lesson.

Then there are the conditions that matches are played in. Snow, ice, rain, mud. In England the game goes on.

In Yugoslavia you wouldn't get many people to watch if you tried to play in these conditions!

In my country spectators like to watch in comfort and they want the best conditions for the players. We don't try to play football between December and February. And we have a much warmer climate than in England to start with!

Another object of the English game that takes some getting used to is the way you treat the goalkeepers.

In Yugoslavia if a forward goes near the goalkeeper it's a free-kick. When I first played for Chelsea I was really shocked. Time after time I was injured. I thought to myself—'This is not football.' Every game it was like a war.

Now I am used to it. I have to talk to myself all the time in

ENGLISH 'KEEPERS HAVE TO BE BEST IN THE WORLD

a game. ' Keep calm, count to ten. Look this way, look that way.' For ninety minutes I have to concentrate on every move.

I am mentally exhausted after every game. I don't sleep until four or five o'clock in the mornings. In Yugoslavia I could sleep for much of the match!

Here it's action all the time. I can't relax for one second. That's why English goalkeepers are best in the world. They have to be!

Yugoslavia have a reputation for producing good 'keepers. Pantelic, Radenkovic, Cjurkovic have all done well for other European clubs.

But until you play in the English League you can't call yourself a goalkeeper. It's the toughest place to be the last line of defence.

Peter Shilton and Ray Clemence are world class. But another British goalkeeper's the best of all. That's Pat Jennings.

I asked Arsenal this year if I could train for two weeks with Pat Jennings because I wanted to learn from him. Pat always seems to be in the right place to make saves.

Settling down in English football has been hard for me. but I have loved it with Chelsea.

One reason is that, to me, English football is the most entertaining in the world. It's exciting to play in and to watch.

In Yugoslavia, Italy and in most European countries the style is very different. It's very slow build-up, very patient, very cautious, but not very exciting for fans.

In England it's fast all the time. Play swings from one end to the other. When I first came, I found it confusing. Everyone crowded in the goalmouth making it difficult for the goalkeeper to know what was happening.

It's the outfield play that makes the goalkeeping different in England to my country.

In Yugoslavia it's normal for the goalkeeper to play like a sweeper. To come out of the penalty area to play the ball.

**GEOFF HURST—
had his doubts**

Here it is not so usual and when I do it, people think I'm a bit of a clown.

Geoff Hurst, the Chelsea manager at that time, had some doubts about my style. He tried to get me to change and play like English goalkeepers. We talked it over a lot. Geoff wanted me to stop playing my natural game but I wasn't keen.

I told him, ' I know what I'm doing. This is the way I play. I'm no clown.'

I like to make the fans enjoy the game, but I still play very seriously. I don't do anything just for the fans. I try to be very professional on and off the pitch.

I have signed a new contract with Chelsea this' year because I love the club and want to continue to play here. I had approaches from New York Cosmos but I didn't like the idea of playing in America at this time.

Right now I like it in London and my wife Biba and my daughters, Marala, 6, and Barbara, 4, are settled. My girls speak better English than me.

When I first arrived in London I went to classes to learn English but I didn't do very well. I was too tired after training and playing to learn a new language.

I've just had to pick it up from television and newspapers. The other players make jokes all the time about my English and I laugh, too.

London is much, much bigger than Belgrade and everything goes so fast. There seems to be little time to talk to people. Everybody is rushing here or rushing there—it's like the football.

You might think your footballers here are not as skilful as those in other countries. That's quite wrong.

I think English footballers have just as much skill and control as those on the Continent. But the game is played so fast in England, the players have less chance to show their skills.

To demonstrate skill at high speed needs incredible ability. Continental players look better because they do things more slowly.

I think in English football are some of the best young players in the world—Glenn Hoddle, Gary Shaw, Russell Osman and many others.

A World Cup without England is not a good competition. England are the kings of football even if they are no longer champions of the world. You have the players but you handicap them by playing so many matches.

Plus, every other country loves to play against England. They always give 120 percent against England. It's every foreign player's ambition to play England at Wembley.

I felt the same when I played for Yugoslavia. I won 14 full caps and was captain three times. I have wonderful memories from the Munich World Cup in 1974.

Miljan Miljanic asked me if I wanted to be in the squad for the current World Cup matches but I believed it was not fair to Chelsea.

But England should be there. They have some of the best players despite their crazy way of playing the game.

AWAY GOES ARCHIE!

With Manchester United's SAMMY McILROY grounded, Birmingham City's pocket-sized powerhouse ARCHIE GEMMILL pounces on the ball and heads for goal.

HEY, REF!

■ There's no doubt that Q.P.R.'s IAN GILLARD is really up-tight about something — and the reason was this tackle by Newcastle's Stuart Boam on Gary Waddock. Ian's appeals were answered — the ref awarded a free-kick.

21

You need

That's the message from these pics of close quarter battles

TOMMY CATON (Man. City) climbs above Leeds' ARTHUR GRAHAM

GARTH CROOKS (Spurs) in the grip of Arsenal's WILLIE YOUNG

Leicester's ANDY PEAKE (left) challenges Sunderland's KEVIN ARNOTT

hands...

IAN BAILEY (Middlesbrough) holds back KEVIN REEVES (Manchester City).

Sunderland's GORDON CHISHOLM puts an arm lock on KEVIN KEEGAN (Southampton)

STEVE WILLIAMS (Southampton) puts a restraining hand on Spurs' RICCY VILLA

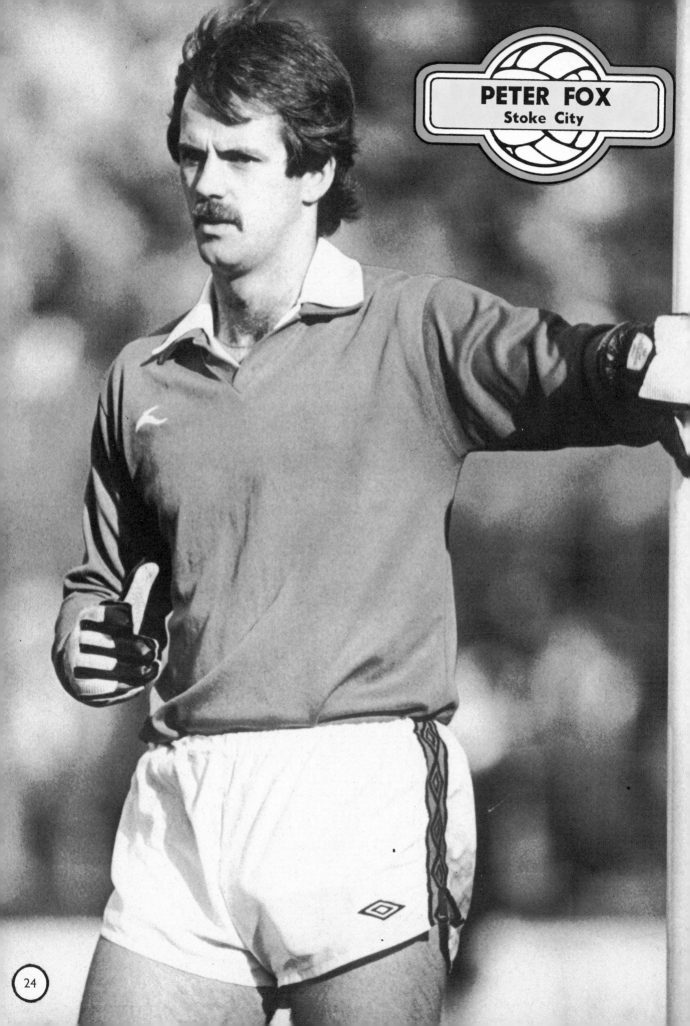

PETER FOX
Stoke City

24

ALL SMILES...
Terry McDermott's pleasure is shared by his jubilant England team-mates.

...AND THIS IS WHY
This cracking goal scored by the Liverpool star against Norway.

THERE is one time in the week when you might think I had fallen out with my Leeds United team-mates. It happens at Saturday lunch-times when my Elland Road pals fall about in fits of laughter as they watch the television preview of the day's football action.

What makes the Leeds lads double up with laughter are the antics and errors of Scottish goalkeepers. But I sit tight-lipped and unsmiling.

I'm aware that soon I might be having the kind of nightmare afternoon my team-mates have been laughing at.

Although I'm still only 21 I've already had my share of bad times. The days when you think you have a simple shot covered only for the ball to spin off your hand into the net.

Coventry beat us in the replay my error had been really punished.

It was then Leeds boss Allan Clarke came into his own. He steadfastly stood by me, insisting I had the ability to become England's goalie in the future. He had the utmost faith in me.

He told me he had no intention of dropping me. It was up to me to battle my way back to form.

I realise now what a great favour Mr Clarke did for me. If I had dropped out of the first team reckoning I would only have been hiding. Eventually the pressure would be back on me and I would have to keep goal in front of my critics.

The turning point came later on a League visit to White Hart Lane.

-NO PLACE

I took a lot of criticism last term. After establishing myself in the Leeds side and winning England Under-21 honours I hit a bad patch.

After losing 5-0 at Elland Road against Arsenal I left the field in tears. I had turned a cross from John Hollins into my own net for the Gunners' first goal. Their third went between my legs, the final indignity for a 'keeper.

Immediately I was under pressure. Folk who had rated me highly began to criticise me. They seized on my slightest mistake.

I had a string of poor performances and hit a real low in our F.A. Cup third round tie against Coventry City. We were leading City by the only score when I let in a soft goal to give Coventry a draw. I was shattered.

After the game I was bitterly upset. I had let down my team-mates and the Leeds fans. When

I had a fine game in front of the television cameras but I can let you into a secret now.

My saves from Tottenham Hotspur's Glenn Hoddle were shown in slow-motion, action-replays. They silenced the folk who had knocked me, yet I found those saves relatively easy to make.

You see, when a player like Hoddle receives the ball anywhere near goal a 'keeper is always on his toes. I was so aware of Glenn's shooting power I would have been angry with myself if I'd let one of his efforts in. After the Spurs outing my confidence began to return.

When I was really down in the dumps I would wake up at night asking myself why I had made a mistake. Constantly I tried to analyse my errors. Yet I was never scared of playing in the next game. I always had confidence in my own ability.

It was also a great lift for me to be selected for the Under-21 squads. You might wonder how somebody with a foreign sounding name like mine qualifies to play for England.

I was born in the town that has proved a great breeding ground for goalkeepers— Chesterfield. Both my parents though are Yugoslavs. They moved to Britain over thirty years ago, were married here and set up home in Chesterfield.

Former goalkeepers like Gordon Banks (England), Bob Wilson (Scotland), and now on B.B.C. television, and John Osborne (West Bromwich Albion) were all either born or brought up in my home town. Current League performers like Alan Stevenson (Burnley), Steve Ogrizovic (Liverpool) and Steve Hardwick (Newcastle) also hail from there.

That call-up was a tremendous honour for me. It showed how highly United rated me. And I have to admit I was very happy to become an apprentice and then a professional at Elland Road.

It's amazing though that just in four years as a professional I have played under FOUR different managers.

My first boss was Jimmy Armfield who was sacked. Jock Stein had a brief spell in charge before accepting the task of leading Scotland. Then after Jimmy Adamson, Allan Clarke arrived.

Each of the managers had his own

TO HIDE

Leeds' JOHN LUKIC on the problems of being a goalkeeper

I actually went to the same junior school as Bob Wilson but I was a tough-tackling left-back until our school team goalie failed to turn up for a game. Suddenly I was handed a 'keeper's jersey. I've been wearing one ever since.

I was recommended to Leeds when I was only 13. After trials I signed as a schoolboy. One of the greatest challenges of my life came when I was asked to play for the Leeds reserve team when I was still at school.

ideas on how to work goalkeepers. Most of them brought in their own coaches.

Now I feel one of Allan Clarke's appointments has really proved ideal for me. The present boss brought back former Leeds and Scotland 'keeper David Harvey to work as youth team coach and adviser to the club's goalies.

It's a big help having somebody with David's specialist knowledge around. He spots small things that an outfield player would miss. He pinpoints occasions when by moving perhaps a few feet to one side of my goal I could have prevented a score.

And in Allan Clarke we have one of the greatest strikers of all time. By questioning him I find out how forwards are likely to react in front of goal and what weaknesses they search for in a goalie.

If I continue to work hard and listen to the advice of Dave and Allan I'm sure I can become a better keeper. And one day achieve my ambition of playing for England's senior team.

GLENN HODDLE—
Spurs shooting star

CROSSWORD

ACROSS

1. Portsmouth to their fans. (6)
4. Southampton's Charlie. (6)
9. Mal of many clubs. (7)
10. Ex-England team boss. (5)
11. Wolves' Mel. (4)
12. Resort to dropping part of Wrexham's ground! (8)
15. Leicester Irishman. (5)
16. Jumps after pleas from the fans? (5)
21. They're at home at Oakwell. (8)
23. St Mirren and Scotland forward. (4)
25. Ardiles to his mates. (5)
27. Team always with a heavy burden to carry? (7)
28. Manchester United and Eire player. (6)
29. Kilmarnock manager reversed in clue! (6)

DOWN

1. Performer in a replay? (6)
2. Brighton boss (7)
3. Repeat chant. (4)
5. Make a mistake. (3)
6. Wandering Blackburn player for example. (5)
7. Third Division City. (6)
8. Half of a famous Italian club. (5)
13. West Brom's Gary. (4)
14. Teams toss for choice of it! (4)
17. Team who sound as if they kept going to the end! (7)
18. Shape of a soccer pitch. (6)
19. What Shilton and Barnes have in common. (5)
20. European national team. (6)
22. Italian sharpshooter. (5)
24. Down where Southampton play. (4)
26. Watch with a view to signing? (3)

Answers on page 116

Pat Jennings
SATURDAY SPECIAL

Follow Arsenal 'keeper Pat Jennings as he prepares for a tough First Division fixture. Off-the-field build-up and on-the-field action all go to make Saturday so special for footballers like Pat.

Pat's wife sees him off as he heads for the team meeting.

A nearby golf club provides just the right atmosphere for the players to relax and prepare for the game.

Pat watches Alan Sunderland, Arsenal's answer to Ray Reardon, in action. Willie Young looks on — no doubt hoping this is the only shot Alan will miss today!

Over lunch Pat and the other players talk about the game to come. Their opponents Middlesbrough are never easy to beat — even at Highbury.

After lunch, Pat and his teamates watch the football previews on television. With a bit of luck there may be something on about Middlesbrough which might be useful.

After lunch the players head for Highbury. The autograph hunters are already out in force when Pat arrives.

Pat has a word with manager Terry Neill (left) and trainer Fred Street.

At last the moment Pat and all the other players have been anxiously waiting for.

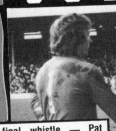

The final whistle — Pat shakes hands with fellow goalkeeper Middlesbrough's JIM PLATT. The game ends in a draw.

A minor injury is bothering Pat, so it's into the treatment room where Fred does his stuff.

As kick-off looms nearer, Pat goes to the dressing-room to get stripped.

Then it's into the gym for a warming up session.

ACTION. The time when the preparation and practice are put to the test.

After the game Pat and the other players relax in the players' lounge. Here he has a word with Middlesbrough's Terry Cochrane and Jim Platt.

The game is long over, but a number of fans are still waiting with their autograph books ready. Another Saturday, the big day of the week for pros like Pat, is nearly over.

SKY HIGH!

That's how th[e]
fans in Everton['s]
main stand mu[st]
feel when they g[et]
this view of the actio[n]

And just to be fair
— this is the view
that the players
get of the
towering
stand.

KENNY SANSOM
Arsenal

33

Odd, amusing and unusual—it all happens in football.

CAUGHT BY THE CAMERA

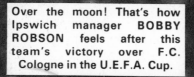

Over the moon! That's how Ipswich manager BOBBY ROBSON feels after this team's victory over F.C. Cologne in the U.E.F.A. Cup.

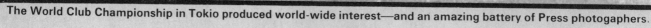

The World Club Championship in Tokio produced world-wide interest—and an amazing battery of Press photogaphers.

How did that get there? Sunderland's ALAN BROWN seems to have a problem on his hands.

England players putting on the style in a training session.

DEREK PARLANE (Leeds) is the unlucky lad on the receiving end of this tackle.

Leicester's LARRY MAY takes on a four-legged opponent. Let's hope its bark is worse than its bite.

Who pinched me barrow? KEVIN KEEGAN (England) left and STEVE HEIGHWAY (Eire) seem to be asking that question.

RAZZAMATAZZ

- ROTHERHAM STYLE!

The most entertaining team ever seen here, said one fan. No, it wasn't Liverpool, Real Madrid or a crack Argentinian outfit — but a group of circus acts giving a pre-match display at the Rotherham v. Brentford game! It certainly brought a touch of razzamatazz to the Third Division ground.

COLIN McADAM
Rangers

37

TESTING TIME

Sharpen your wits on these puzzles and posers

TEN-YEAR QUIZ

Can you name the teams who won the following competitions in the years shown—
1972—European Cup Winners Cup.
1973—English First Division Championship.
1974—World Cup.
1975—European Cup.
1976—UEFA Cup.
1977—English Second Division Championship.
1978—English League Cup.
1979—English Third Division Championship.
1980—Scottish Premier League Championship.
1981—English Fourth Division Championship.

WORLD CUP PLAYERS

Fill in the countries of the following World Cup players—

1 Zoff — *Italy*
2 Vogts — *West Germany,*
3 Oscar — *Brazil*
4 Pirri — *Spain*
5 Neeskens — *Holland*
6 Tardelli — *Italy*
7 Bonhof — *West germany*
8 Platini — *Italy*
9 Lato — *poland*
10 Krankl — *Austria*

FACE NAME

This face is made up of the letters of the name of a famous player.

Dalglish

ODD Spots

1—Which team played in chocolate-coloured shirts as their alternative strip last season?
2—Why is the name St Johnstone unique in British League football?
3—Which teams play at (a) Baseball Ground, (b) Racecourse Ground, (c) Rugby Park?
4—What have Aberdeen and Wimbledon in common?

(ANSWERS ON PAGE 116)

GOALKEEPERS IN HIDING

Spot the names of 12 goalkeepers by using the letters in this diagram, across, down, up, backwards, or diagonally.

S	Y	V	R	H	T	Y	L	B	A	R	S
A	P	E	N	O	T	L	I	H	S	E	E
T	T	A	L	P	U	O	T	E	K	P	K
J	E	N	N	I	N	G	S	A	N	O	R
D	O	O	W	Y	A	D	H	N	U	O	A
N	E	D	D	O	G	B	R	O	T	C	P

38

UNDER PRESSURE!

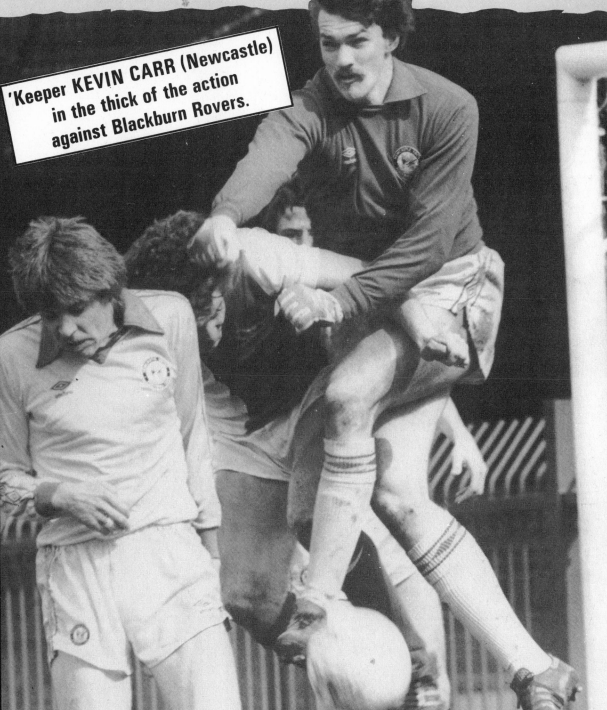

'Keeper KEVIN CARR (Newcastle) in the thick of the action against Blackburn Rovers.

JOHN WENT ON AND ON AND ON...

JOHN TROLLOPE has 770 programmes from the League matches he played for Swindon Town. But there is one that holds pride of place. The day Third Division Swindon Town went to Wembley and beat mighty Arsenal 3-1 in the League Cup Final in 1968-69 season.

"That has to be the high point of my career," says John. "But I'll always remember the 770 League games. I have a programme to remind me of every one."

Now the manager of Swindon Town, he began his career as a 17-year-old full back, before going on to notch up his incredible tally of appearances.

Until John Trollope, the player who held the record for the most League appearances with one club was Jimmy Dickinson, Portsmouth. Jimmy played 764 League games for Portsmouth, won 49 England caps and played in two championship-winning teams with the south coast club.

When Trollope beat Dickinson's record he received a Mecca Loyalty Award trophy from the ex-Portsmouth man.

"I didn't think my total would be beaten," said Jimmy. "To achieve such a record a current player would have to steer clear of injuries, maintain a consistent standard of performance, and not miss a match for 17 seasons."

An almost impossible modern day feat.

John Trollope never won the honours that went to Jimmy Dickinson, but he holds an almost unbeatable record. Plus programmes from every match to prove it.

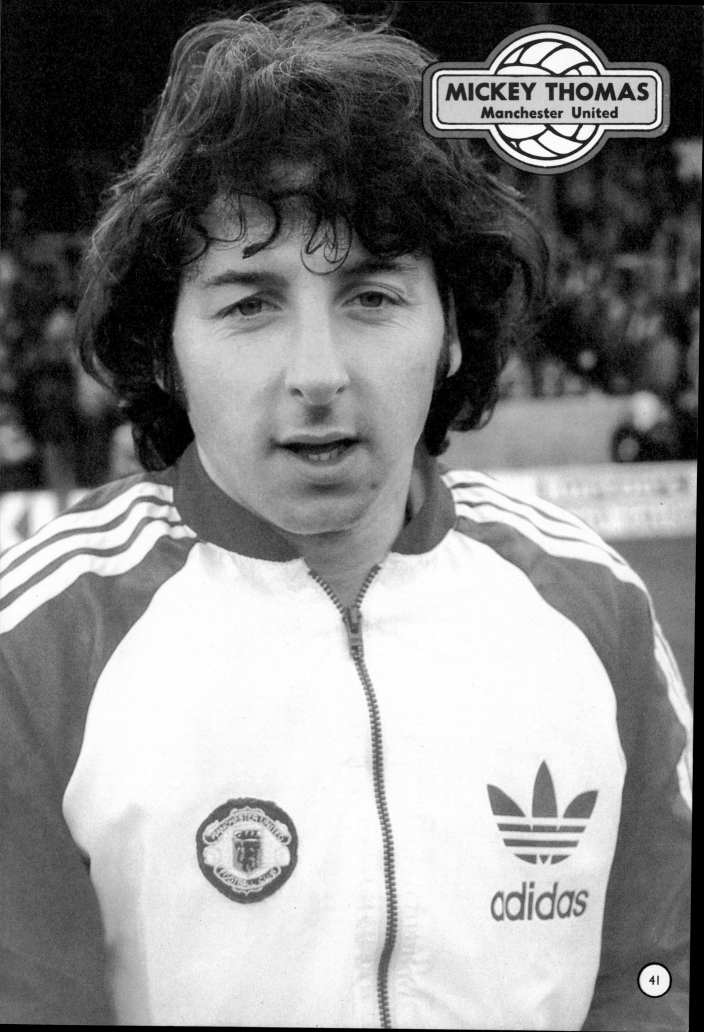

MICKEY THOMAS
Manchester United

41

THAT WAS SOME YEAR!

THE last year has been an incredible experience for me.

I suppose the best way to sum it up is that at the beginning of it, I was teaching the aristocracy to play football— now the football aristocracy is teaching me!

Little more than a year ago I was just another Second Division player with Queen's Park Rangers. In my spare afternoons I coached youngsters at the famous public school, Harrow.

Then out of the blue came a transfer to West Ham United—and a different world. European competition, a League Cup final against Liverpool—and finally promotion to the First Division.

I gave up the coaching assignment to do some learning myself from the best players in the world. I hope it's paying off.

The memories of last season will do a lifetime.

Walking out at Wembley for the League Cup final and seeing the mass of West Ham colours was unforgettable. Scoring in the replay at Villa Park was as memorable, even if we eventually lost the game.

Playing our Cup Winners' Cup ties in Spain, Rumania and Russia all provided me with moments to look back on.

It's been such a great year and a half I go cold at the thought that I nearly didn't take up football at all!

As a schoolboy I was attached to Queen's Park Rangers, and they wanted me to become an apprentice. But my parents were not so keen. They wanted me to carry on with my studies and go on to teachers' training college.

I was undecided. My parents left it up to me—and I chose to gamble on football.

But I promised that if I hadn't established myself by the age of 21 I would quit football and go into teaching.

No danger of that now! I felt I established myself with Rangers when I was 20, and I was already at West Ham following an £800,000 transfer when my ' deadline ' of my 21st birthday came.

It was with Rangers that the opportunity to coach at Harrow came up. It was quite an experience.

For a start the boys at Harrow couldn't play! At 16 years old they were the standard of 12-year-olds anywhere else.

They were only just starting to play soccer at the school. It had all been rugby or Harrow football which is a mixture of rugby and soccer.

The other problem was the names. Lord so-and-so, or the Hon. somebody, or some foreign names I couldn't pronounce. After one week I gave up proper names and gave all the boys a nickname I could remember.

But they still called me ' Mr Goddard.' I stayed 2½ years at Harrow coaching one afternoon a week. It was enjoyable, even if the standard wasn't great.

I had to give it up when I joined West Ham, because of the travel involved across London.

Talk of travel brings me to the Cup Winners' Cup matches last season, my first taste of foreign competition.

42

West Ham's PAUL GODDARD looks back

The different games provided an odd contrast. In the home leg of our first round tie against Castilla of Spain we were forced to play the match behind closed doors due to trouble involving some of our fans in Madrid.

There was a grand total of 262 people inside the ground, making things seem really weird.

But the amazing thing was those 262—coaches, trainers, officials, TV and press reporters and cameramen—seemed to make more noise than the crowd in a game we played in Russia. And that was 85,000!

The Castilla match created a strange atmosphere. It was unreal to play a very important match without a crowd.

The contrast in Tbilisi in Russia was amazing. The stadium was packed solid. Up to that point it was the biggest crowd I'd ever played in front of—and the quietest.

They gave us a great reception when we took the field but during play you could almost hear a pin drop. It was strange—as if they were ordered not to cheer.

The entire trip to Russia was one I'll never forget. It was one long 'hassle'. We had to fly to Tbilisi, in Georgia, via Moscow. And that's where the trouble started. They told us that snowfalls prevented our connecting flight from taking off.

They took ages to study every passport—and with 16 players, plus officials and press men in the party the delays were considerable.

It was a trip when you either felt like laughing or crying, and footballers usually end up laughing.

There are jokers in every team, and at West Ham we have David Cross. He has a dry sense of humour and an amazing store of general knowledge.

The funniest thing was on a journey back from Spain. We got into the customs hall at the airport to find a tremendous scrummage round the baggage turntable.

There was no way we could get near it to pick up our cases. Next minute Crossie had taken off his jacket and buttoned it up with one arm inside. He stood there like a one-armed man, and everybody made way for him. He picked up his case no problem!

David also proved a great team-mate for me to play alongside. He works so hard off the ball helping to make space, and wins so much in the air I found it easy to play with him.

All the matches and the travelling with West Ham in the last year, has forced me to cut down on another outside interest—the Boys' Brigade.

My father is a Captain in the Southall Regiment, and I have been brought up as a member of the Brigade.

I've always taken a bit of a ribbing from the other players about my involvement—at West Ham they call me ' Sarge '—but the Boys' Brigade has meant a lot to me.

It has given me fellowship and friendship that I will always value. At Southall we have members from all races—English, West Indian, Asians, Africans—and there is never any bother.

I have reached the rank of Warrant Officer, and when I have the time I take the boys for football and gymnastics.

I like to have an interest outside the game. To have somewhere to relax, even though I am enjoying my football with West Ham more than at any time since I was at school.

You never know what is round the corner in football. Things have gone so well for me I keep expecting something to go wrong.

I just hope it doesn't because I want to enjoy my first season in the First Division—along with the soccer's toffs.

DAVID CROSS — goalscorer and team laughter-maker.

TALENTED TWOSOME

Showing that footballers have skills off the pitch are Mark Wallington and Kenny Clements.

Oldham defender Kenny Clements proves he's no mean artist with this selection of Disney characters in his son Antony's bedroom.

Mark, Leicester skipper and keeper, has made a name for himself with his gardening, winning quite a few medals with his champion veg.

EDDIE GRAY
Leeds United

GLOVES FOR EVERY OCCASION

Be prepared—that must be the motto of Villa 'keeper JIMMY RIMMER.

When he takes the field he carries a bag of gloves, a dozen in number—all sorts and shapes and every one designed for a particular use, depending on the conditions.

As the last line of defence for the champions it seems that such careful preparation has paid off for big Jim.

LOU MACARI
Manchester United

KEVIN ARNOTT
Sunderland

48

BIG AND AWKWARD —THAT'S ME!

YOU might think that being six feet four inches tall is a big advantage for a central defender. That it solves all my problems on the pitch.

But playing in the First Division is not just a question of standing in front of goal and heading away high balls.

Being so tall has its advantages—but I can give you at least three reasons why it can also create problems.

Firstly, very tall players like myself have a 'balance' problem. Secondly I have the scars to show that tall players often come off worst in challenges for the ball. And thirdly there's the difficult matter of finding a bed to fit me on our travels!

I have had to work overtime at Ipswich to overcome the clumsiness that comes from being so tall. I don't have the balance or footwork of smaller men.

I'm quick enough running forward but I've had to work on overcoming slowness on the turn. Nippy fowards have always been a problem for me.

I lacked the balance to be able to jockey a nimble-footed striker who was prepared to push the ball past me and run.

As a youngster at Ipswich I thought I would never master the art.

I have to thank coach Bobby Ferguson for putting in so much time on me in training. I owe a debt to Bobby—and I never thought I would ever say that!

He put me through it so much I wanted to get away from Ipswich at one time.

The names he called me in training! 'Camel', 'Crab' and a lot more I can't repeat!

All the harsh words from the coaches got me down—but I stuck at it. And in the end hard work did the trick.

I feel now I have reasonable control for a big chap—but I'm still working to improve.

Last season I became friendly with a boxer named Rory Burke. I was fascinated by his skipping routines in training—and he volunteered to teach them to me.

I'm sure some people would call me a pansy for taking up skipping, but it was all aimed at improving my footwork.

Injuries of course are second nature to a central defender. You expect to get knocks in every match.

Going for high balls I'm obviously at an advantage being so tall. But I seem to get more

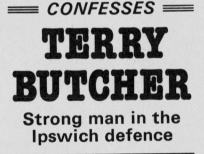

=== CONFESSES ===

TERRY BUTCHER

Strong man in the Ipswich defence

than my share of facial injuries—perhaps because strikers have to jump for balls I can head without leaving the ground.

My understanding with Russell Osman in the Ipswich defence dates back to a facial injury in an England Under-21 match.

Russell and I were playing together for England against Denmark at Watford when we both went up for the same high ball. I ended up with a cut head and Russell a cut nose—and we decided we ought to get a better understanding between us!

We have worked hard to establish our understanding. These days we seldom find ourselves jumping for the same ball.

It's a partnership built up over the years. We were in the youth side and the reserves together at Ipswich—although Russell was always one step ahead of me, despite being younger.

Russell signed as an apprentice with the club at 16, and was already doing well by the time I joined at 17 as a professional.

He won promotion from youth team to reserves and reserves to first team ahead of me, but I always managed to catch him up.

It was a thrill for both of us when we played against Spain last season. It had been a big ambition of ours to play together for the full England side.

We had had one

PRE-MATCH SHOCK FOR IPSWICH IN EUROPE

international appearance before that—against Australia last year. With all due respect to them I don't rate it as a full cap because none of the England senior players was available.

Going to Australia for one

**RUSSELL OSMAN —
building an understanding**

match was quite an experience but not one I'd want to repeat. There was a 26-hour plane journey in each direction, and I felt the effects of that for days afterwards.

As usual on both England and Ipswich trips I roomed with Russell. And in Sydney as everywhere else we had our usual race for the hotel room key.

Whoever gets the key first has first pick of the beds—and that's where the third problem with my height comes in.

I've been all over the world with Ipswich and England teams—and I've never yet found a comfortable hotel bed!

They are all too short! Most of the time my legs dangle out of the end and I wake in the morning with 'dead' calf muscles.

In Sydney the hotel room had a double bed and a couch.

Russell got to reception first, claimed the key—and naturally grabbed the bed, leaving me with the couch.

But the way everything was positioned in the room he slept with my feet virtually in his ear—not a pretty sight!

MEMORABLE JOURNEY

■ I've had some memorable trips into Europe with Ipswich. The highlight perhaps was our UEFA Cup tie against Widzew Lodz in Poland last season.

We took a 5-0 lead from the first leg to Poland—but no way were we complacent about it. It was about 20 degrees below freezing in Lodz, and nobody knew what to expect.

We trained before the match on a pitch with a covering of snow which made football possible. What a shock we got when we turned up at the stadium for the game itself!

The pitch had been swept clean—leaving a sheet of ice! Robin Cousins could have played for us!

It's the only time the Ipswich coaches have ever told us not to even think about trying to play

football—just to belt the ball out of sight.

There could easily have been a freak result—like losing 6-0 —but we got away with a 1-0 defeat that gave us a comfortable aggregate win.

But the most memorable part of the trip was yet to come. We had a three-hour coach drive to the airport. The windows of the coach were iced up solid inside and outside, and the road was like a skating rink.

It could have been nasty. But big Allan Hunter started to sing Christmas carols—it was mid-December—and soon everyone joined in. We spent the entire journey singing carols, I will never forget it. It was a really fantastic feeling. You certainly see life on these trips.

I've seen a bit of life nearer home that others never get to see. Life behind bars! In fact I've played several football matches in prison!

It's ok—I've never been in trouble. It's just that my father is a prison officer at Blundeston Prison in Suffolk, and before I established myself at Ipswich I turned out for the Prison Officers' team.

I've played at Norwich Prison and one or two others as well as at Blundeston. There's a nationwide cup competition for Prison Officers' teams.

My dad first heard of my debut for Ipswich when prisoners heard the news on Radio Orwell and told him. Now I have a lot of fans inside the prison, and they keep my parents supplied with cuttings for the scrapbooks they keep on my career.

They have filled several books already—and I hope there will be plenty more to come.

I feel Ipswich has the kind of set-up and atmosphere which could produce a winning side for a long time to come. The spirit amongst the side is marvellous, and our success should help to attract more top youngsters.

I'm glad I stuck out the hard times at Ipswich. The good times are great.

MIKE ROBINSON
Brighton

51

OUCH! No doubt about how PAUL MARINER, Ipswich, felt after this no-holds-barred clash with Liverpool's RAY KENNEDY.

ANDY GRAY
Wolves

53

LAST-GASP GREENHOFF

A header by Everton's
Bob Latchford looked
a certain scorer —

till Leeds defender
BRIAN GREENHOFF
did his jack-in-the-box
rescue act.

DREW JARVIE
Aberdeen

55

NIGHTMARE –
all because of a holiday!

EVERY morning when I get up, my ankle cracks loudly. As I walk round the room it clicks with every step.

But I don't rush to the telephone to tell Everton physio Jim McGregor to prepare the treatment table for me. Because it is something I have lived with now for nearly four years.

That noise is a constant reminder of how lucky I am to be still playing football. It is a legacy of a disease that could have completely wrecked my football career.

The story goes back to my days at Queen's Park Rangers.

The then manager Frank Sibley took us off for a mid-season break to Marbella in Spain in January 1978. A couple of weeks after our return I awoke one morning to find my ankle was slightly swollen.

I decided I might be able to run it off, so I took part in our normal training session. But my ankle became even more inflamed.

The next day I visited Rangers' physio Richard Roberts and by then my ankle had enlarged to the size of a football. His first question was had I gone over on my ankle recently?

That thought had crossed my mind, but I was quite sure I hadn't injured the ankle in any way.

The physio was as mystified as I was and as my ankle continued to swell he decided to call in the club doctor. Within hours I was being seen by a specialist.

I had various tests but nobody was able to tell me what exactly was wrong. It took a fortnight before a reason for my problem was found.

In the meantime my ankle was slowly getting bigger and the problem had spread to my left knee. That was swelling to the size of a balloon. I was even getting slight twinges in my shoulder.

It was absolutely frightening. Finally the specialist told me I had contracted Reiters Disease. I had probably picked up the virus in Spain.

It's a disease which can deform the joints. I was assured that only happens in really bad cases. Mine was a fairly mild attack, although it still put me out of the game for six months.

DEPTHS OF DESPAIR

■ Without doubt it was one of the most depressing periods of my life. The worst thing was I couldn't bring myself to go to Loftus Road. There wasn't any treatment I could get there anyway.

I would sit for hours on end looking at my knee and ankle, praying the swelling would go down.

But the only real way to find out if the treatment was working was by having blood tests. Gradually the swelling on the joints disappeared and I could walk normally again.

I recovered well and within ten months of being in the depths of despair I achieved a career ambition by joining one of the country's top clubs.

Queen's Park Rangers wanted Everton's Mickey Walsh and Everton manager Gordon Lee was after my services so we both moved in an exchange deal. I was valued at £250,000.

Unfortunately, I didn't get off to the best of starts at Goodison. The move to such a well-respected outfit affected my confidence badly.

For the whole of 1979 I didn't score one goal. I began to wonder if I would ever succeed at Everton. However, the fact I couldn't hit the back of the net was compensated for by working

very hard in my general play.

I found the fans took to me because of that. They saw I was fighting for Everton and consequently I wasn't given a lot of stick about not scoring.

However, I did wonder whether Gordon Lee would also continue to see it that way. I thought a move for me was being considered. But I battled on, determined I was going to do something with my career.

I calmed down in front of goal and stopped snatching at chances. Soon the goals started arriving.

Probably the best thing I ever did in my career was to move from First Division Wolverhampton Wanderers to Third Division Swindon Town.

Dropping two divisions sounds a drastic step backwards. But I viewed the transfer as a roundabout way to a secure place in Division One.

I was 20 when I made up my mind to go. There were plenty of lads of my age who were regulars in other First Division sides, but I wasn't getting very far at Molineux. John Richards and Derek Dougan had the striking positions well sewn up. I only got in for the odd match when they were injured.

I was also a quiet lad. I was a bag of nerves whenever I got my chance. I regret being too quiet now. If I had had a few more things to say I might have grabbed the headlines and then people would have to take notice of me.

However, the move to Swindon Town away from the star names did me good. I achieved a regular place at the County Ground, scored goals and gained a lot of invaluable self confidence.

If I hadn't left Wolves for Town when I did I'm sure I wouldn't be half the player I am now. My hope that a move from Molineux would eventually win me a place with a First Division club was realised when Queen's Park Rangers signed me in 1976.

I am a little disappointed

JOHN RICHARDS—
he blocked the way

there haven't been too many great highlights in my career. I can't point to any medal to show what I have achieved. But that terrifying period of my life during 1978 always makes the few high spots even better.

And when I do hit any bad patches—that tell-tale click, click, click always makes me thankful I am still able to get out there on the pitch at all!

DAVE BENNETT
Manchester City

HEADING FOR A FALL

European football can be rough and tough as Ipswich's **ERIC GATES** found in this clash with Zdenek Prokes of Bohemians Prague.

ALL-OUT!

All in a tangle are ANDY GRAY (Wolves) left and PAUL DYSON (Coventry).

Power in the air as JOE GALLAGHER (Birmingham) beats LEE CHAPMAN (Stoke) in the jump.

ALVIN MARTIN (West Ham) soars above Watford's WILF ROSTRON.

Muscle-stretching action caught by the camera

This high-flying trio are from l. to r. JOE MAYO, Orient, and Preston's BRIAN TAYLOR and MICK BAXTER.

Arsenal's BRIAN TALBOT puts the pressure on to reach a high ball.

NEVER GIVE UP!

Frank advice from West Brom's powerhouse midfielder, REMI MOSES

I HAVE a message for all youngsters who think they have enough talent to be professional footballers but who can't persuade a club to take them on. Never give up!

As a teenager I was a regular in the Manchester Boys' side. An outfit often watched by talent scouts from big name clubs. I was an established member of the set-up so I must have been a fair player.

Unfortunately almost every scout came up with the same verdict on me. At 5' 3" I was too small.

Glamour outfits like Manchester City and Manchester United were just not interested. I even wrote to lesser teams like Oldham Athletic and Stockport County asking them to watch me or give me a trial. But they agreed with the general view—I had no chance of making the grade because I was a ' titch '.

My big breakthrough came when just one man had faith in me. And he had contacts in the right places. That man was Tom Corless. He liked my all-action style. Said my lack of inches didn't bother him, so he recommended me to West Bromwich Albion.

Albion invited me to the Hawthorns for trials and quickly signed me, first as a schoolboy, then as an apprentice.

To me it seemed like the first step on the ladder to success. I was born and brought up in a rough area of Manchester called Miles Platting. There are only two ways to get out of there and be a success. One is as a boxer. The other . . . become a top class footballer.

I did try my hand at boxing. But I lost my temper when I was punched. You have to have self-discipline to be a boxer. If you lose your cool and chase blindly after your opponent you are asking to be beaten.

After just one week in the gym I decided to hang up my gloves and concentrate on making the grade in football!

Many youngsters go off the rails in Miles Platting because there's so little for them to do and nobody takes any interest in them.

I was fortunate my parents were really keen for me to get some qualifications. They desperately wanted me to be a car mechanic. But I became determined to prove my worth as a footballer.

And I reckon the attitude that helped me make the grade then is still with me as a First Division performer and England Under-21 international now.

I worked hard to make the grade and now I value my success. Playing for West Brom

" THE BEST PLAYER I'VE EVER SEEN "

has given me the earning power and life-style I could only dream of as a boy.

I don't intend to make any mistakes now. For instance, when the first team gets a day off I invariably turn up to train with the reserves and apprentices.

I was also very fortunate at Albion to be signed by their former player-manager Johnny Giles.

I watched Mr Giles (now coach at Vancouver Whitecaps) on many occasions. He was near the end of his playing career after spending the best part of his life with Leeds United. But even in his mid-thirties 'Gilesy' was absolutely brilliant.

He made things look so simple. He had a beautiful touch and could instantly trap a ball and hit inch-perfect passes. As I gain experience my opinion of John becomes even greater. He's the best player I've ever seen.

As well as being a brilliant passer Giles could also win tackles. An aspect of the game I reckon I'm good at.

I've grown since I was a teenager. I'm now 5' 7" and quite stockily built. And I enjoy winning the ball in the midfield engine room.

The great thing about being a ball-winner is that when things are going badly for me in a game I just concentrate on my tackling. I don't allow a few wayward passes to rattle me. After winning a few tackles I can force my way back into a game.

I get my unusual name from my father. He comes from Lagos in Nigeria. But he moved to England many years ago and I was born and bred in Manchester.

I'm certain though it has been easy for me to settle at West Brom because I am fourth in the line of black players to do well there.

BRENDON BATSON —
full-back with a future

Laurie Cunningham (now Real Madrid) and Cyrille Regis were the first on the scene. They were quickly joined by England 'B' international full-back Brendon Batson.

We have a large following of coloured youngsters. And seeing the black men in the team must be a big boost to them. Gives them something to aim for in the future.

I'm very optimistic and excited about my future. I've made the breakthrough into international action. And the West Brom side is packed with young players.

If we hit peak form over the next two or three seasons a host of silverware could end up in Albion's trophy cabinet. And I hope a young man dismissed by many clubs as " too small " will have played a major role in that success.

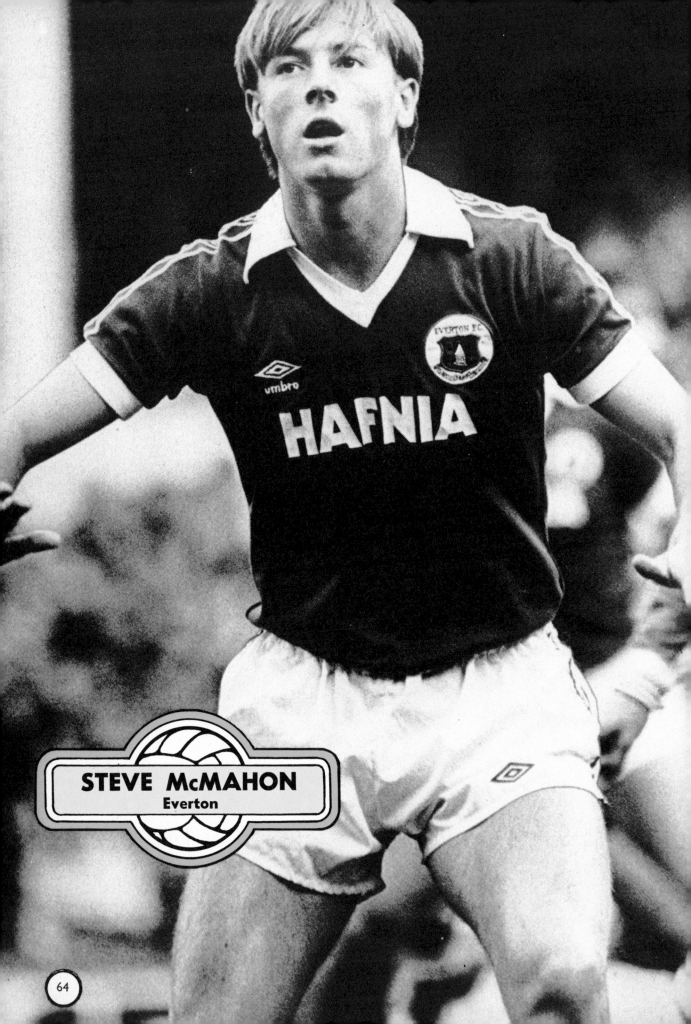

STEVE McMAHON
Everton

TOMMY CATON
Manchester City

GOOD CAPTAINS ARE BORN, NOT MADE!
That's ALAN MULLERY talking

ALAN MULLERY was an outstanding modern captain. Skipper of Spurs, Fulham and England, he led sides in the finals of the F.A. Cup, the Football League Cup and the U.E.F.A Cup.

He was a captain who was always in the thick of the action. Driving, making himself heard, demanding more and more from his team.

So there's no doubt that the present day Brighton manager has the right credentials to talk about what makes a good captain.

"First, I'm convinced that captains are born, not made.

"As a manager, I'll go out and buy a player—to cover a particular position. I don't think I'll ever be able to say 'I'll buy a captain.' A captain has to have character and authority.

"I think if you look at any captain, of any club, you will find they have always been a captain. They have been leaders since they were six or seven years old.

"The person that every other lad turned to. The driver on the field.

"Some captains lead by example. Some lead by shouting. But they all have character and authority. The rest of the side look to them when things are going wrong.

"In my playing day there were several outstanding skippers such as Danny Blanchflower (Spurs and Northern Ireland); Bobby Moore (West Ham Utd. and England); Dave Mackay (Spurs and Scotland); Frank McLintock (Arsenal). Yet each was so different.

"Danny Blanchflower was the quiet man who had so much authority on the field. When I arrived at 'Spurs I was told the story of how Danny Blanchflower resigned as captain because he did not have full authority on the field. He maintained he had been signed from Aston Villa not just as a

66

A SKIPPER HAS TO BE A MID-FIELD PLAYER

mid-field player but to take over from Sir Alf Ramsey as captain at White Hart Lane.

" You rarely heard Danny on the field. But he still had tremendous authority and character.

" When Danny left there was Dave Mackay—a very different kind of captain. Chest stuck out, his was a real wanting-to-win-every-ball attitude, and he expected the same from every other player in the team.

" Bobby Moore was a great example of the quiet man approach. He never seemed to be under any pressure. On the field he showed the same attitude as team manager, Sir Alf Ramsey off the field. But despite the calmness and coolness he commanded the respect of every player in the team.

" And that is something that every captain must do.

" Of the current players I don't think there is a better skipper than Mick Mills (Ipswich). He combines the best qualities of Bobby Moore and Dave Mackay—quiet but still demanding.

" Brian Horton, my skipper at Brighton, is in the same mould.

" He's my voice on the pitch.

" I've always felt that a good

BRIAN HORTON

captain can help make a team.

" And it does not mean that he has to always carry the ball out at the start of a match. Alan Ball has always been a leader on the field. He does not have to be a captain to lead.

" Arsenal made John Hollins skipper when David O'Leary was out of the side last season. John Hollins has always been captain material.

" At the same time that Arsenal were looking for a skipper to fill in for David O'Leary they gave the job to Pat Jennings.

DENNIS MORTIMER

" But the Irish international-ist is a goalkeeper, and I don't think even the greatest 'keeper in the world should be a captain.

" A skipper really has to be a mid-field player. How can a goalkeeper organise things for a free kick, or a corner kick, in the opposition penalty area?

" The same applies to an out-and-out striker. He can't be back organising his defence. It has to be a player who is always involved in the game—for ninety minutes.

BILLY BONDS

" Pat Jennings is a quiet man at the best of times, but even if he had the loudest voice on the field, I don't think a 'keeper should be skipper—even such a respected player like Pat Jennings.

" Dennis Mortimer (Aston Villa) and Billy Bonds (West Ham Utd.) were two of the outstanding skippers last season. Leading from the front and challenging every other player in their team to match their standard of performance.

" Captaincy is one of the weaknesses in the present England team.

" I honestly don't think England have a player who is an automatic skipper at the moment, certainly no one of the stature of Bobby Moore.

" It's another problem we have to solve if we want to become a world class power. We certainly can't make one.

" Captains are born. They have to lead. They have to have character and authority, and have the confidence to make their own decision out there on the pitch where it's all happening."

KEITH BERTSCHIN
Birmingham City

TREVOR BROOKING
West Ham United

69

CASUALTY CORNER

No lack of help for Villa's KEN MCNAUGHT as he's carried off after injuring his knee against Manchester City.

MR COURAGE—Wolves PETER DANIEL manages to walk off the pitch unaided, despite a broken leg.

Stretchered off! Manchester City's PHIL BOYER is the injured player here.

PAUL MARINER (Ipswich) hits the deck after being injured in a heading duel.

No doubt about how MARK LAWRENSON (Brighton) feels after sustaining a back injury.

GRAEME SOUNESS
Liverpool

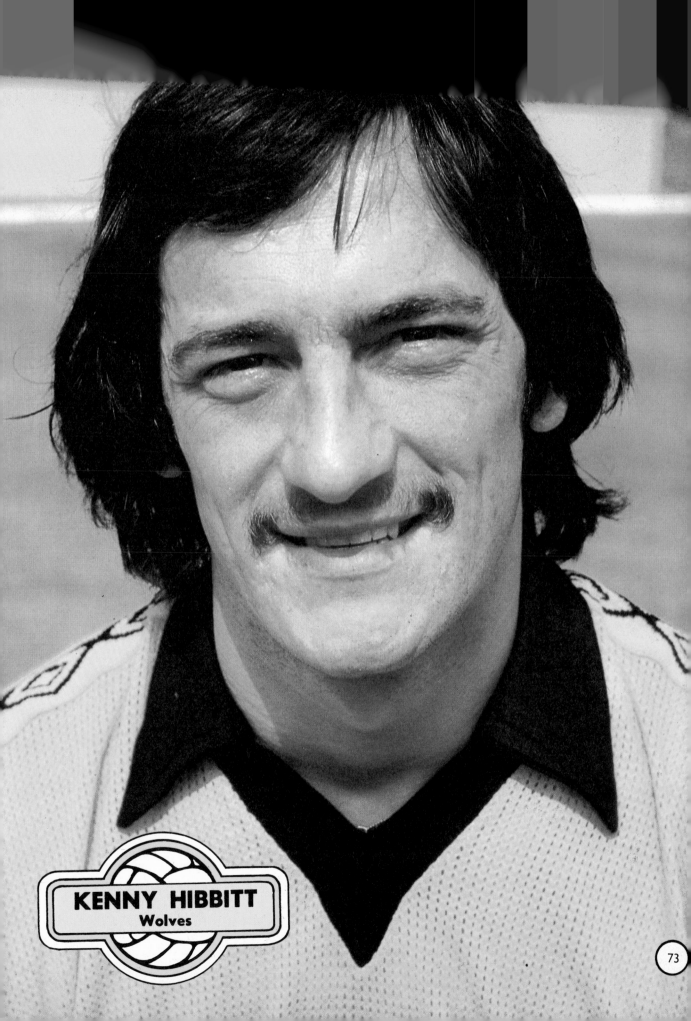

KENNY HIBBITT
Wolves

73

It's the best moment in Football

—SAYS KENNY BURNS (NOTTINGHAM FOREST)

DURING my career with Birmingham City and Nottingham Forest, I have played mostly at centre back or centre forward.

Scotland manager Jock Stein has even used me as a midfield man. Which means that a lot of youngsters ask me which position I like best. I always tell them there is a price to pay wherever you are on a football pitch.

I don't know anyone who has ever kicked a ball who doesn't get a thrill out of scoring goals. That has to be the best moment in football.

So if you become a centre half, you won't get very many chances to score. Always patting some other happy fellow on the back! So you choose centre forward and dream of all the headlines your goals are going to attract.

But there is a snag. I played centre forward often enough to know that it is a very painful occupation. Standing there with your back to goal and a big centre back at your heels you are a sitting target.

People tell me I'm a bit of a hard case. All I will say is that I never looked forward to an afternoon playing up the front and getting as many kicks as the ball.

Nobody but a fool enjoys pain and injury. But that is the price you pay for the excitement and the glamour of being a striker.

Deep down I think I am a defender by nature. I hate giving the opposition an easy time. I like to get in fast and hard and weaken their spirit.

But this is World Cup year and I would love to go to Spain with Scotland. Having played in three different positions I should stand a reasonable chance of getting into the squad as a versatile player.

Ideally I would get into the back four but I will settle for any jersey Mr Stein offers me. I think we will do better than some people think. There is a lot of skill in the squad to back up the power.

People say we blew it in Argentina in 1978 but we were still only a goal away from saving our chance of qualifying for the later stages. Spain is much nearer home. We will be at ease there.

We will also have learned a lot from the Argentine—and we are the only home nation to experience the World Cup finals since England played in Mexico in 1970.

That has to give us an edge. We know what to expect.

HELPING HAND!

Referee Worrall gives assistance to Aston Villa's spearhead striker, PETER WITHE

75

Riccy Villa heads for goal — with Joe Hinnigan in hot pursuit.

JUST THE JOB, JOE!

Argentinian World Cup star, RICCY VILLA, had to give second best to Sunderland's JOE HINNIGAN in this clash in a Sunderland-Spurs encounter.

Shoulder to shoulder they race for the ball.

It's the Sunderland man who gets the first foot to the ball.

Grounded, Riccy Villa can only watch as Joe powers off with the ball.

STEVE WALFORD
Norwich City

77

GORDON CHISHOLM
Sunderland

Rangers' JIM BETT on his football travels
My long road to Ibrox

IT'S only 15 miles from my home town of Hamilton, in Lanarkshire, to Ibrox Stadium, home of mighty Glasgow Rangers.

Yet I had to travel that road the long way round—6,000 miles round, in fact.

Now, at the age of 21, I'm with my fifth club and first love—via two European countries, at that!

I was Rangers-daft as a youngster. But the first club to come for me was Dundee, when I was 14. I signed for them on an "S" form but they released me two years later.

After that, I joined a local amateur side, Gartcosh. While I was with them we travelled to Iceland to play Valur Amateurs. Little did I realise the affect that would have on my career!

At the age of 17, I turned to professional football as a part-timer with Airdrie. Although I was playing in the first team, I wasn't happy. I didn't feel my game was improving.

The Icelandic senior side, Valur, expressed an interest in me and although Airdrie weren't keen to let me go (it took seven months and a visit from Valur's chairman), eventually I got my wish.

I also managed to make a little piece of history by becoming the first foreign footballer to play in Iceland, although my career there couldn't have been much shorter.

After only two games and just as I was beginning to get a hold of the language, I was spotted by Belgian side, Lokeren. They had originally been checking on one of my team-mates but decided to sign me, too.

It was difficult at first. The club had to hire a private tutor to teach me Flemish so I could understand my new team-mates!

However, those difficulties were ironed out and I soon made the first team. In my first full season we were pretty successful, winning a U.E.F.A. Cup place. It was then, just as I finally appeared to be settling down, that I once again found myself on the move.

I was on the point of signing a new three-year contract with Lokeren when I was told that Rangers wanted to buy me. I was completely surprised and didn't make a decision immediately.

Eventually, I decided to join them. For one thing, they were my favourite club and for another, I was missing my family in Hamilton.

Thus Rangers manager John Greig got his man for £170,000. But it hasn't all been plain sailing for me.

I got off to a great start at Ibrox. After only a dozen or so games one supporters' club named me as their Player of the Year and another named themselves after me!

Then Scotland boss Jock Stein picked me for the under-21 internationals against Sweden and Denmark. Thereafter, perhaps inevitably, my form took a dip.

To be honest, I was astounded by the difference

between football in Belgium and in the Scottish Premier League. In Belgium, you're allowed more time with the ball and the game is played at a much slower pace.

I think I've come to terms with that now, however. I only hope I can continue my progress with a full Scotland cap.

ANDY BLAIR
Coventry City

TONY McANDREW
Middlesbrough

81

MY MISERY MONTHS

EVERY player dreams of being a member of a championship - chasing team. Battling every week at the top of the First Division.

But that dream turned into a nightmare for me last season. While my Aston Villa team-mates seemed to play out of their skins every week as we raced against and beat Ipswich Town for the title, I was bitterly disappointed with my form.

Wherever Villa played they won rave reviews for their fast, attacking style. But after the opening couple of months of the term I could hardly put a foot right.

Even now I can't put my finger on the reason for my poor form. I saw manager Ron Saunders week after week to discuss my problems but he couldn't explain the cause of my slump. He just told me to keep battling away. If I gave one hundred per cent effort I would keep my place in the side.

At times though things became really bad. I will never forget our home game against Crystal Palace last term. We won 2-1 but I couldn't do anything right. I continually miscontrolled the ball. I was often caught in possession. And I couldn't even hit a simple square pass to a team-mate a few feet away.

My Villa team-mates still pull my leg about that game. I was the best Palace player on the park is one remark I had thrown at me!

My form slump began after I had been called up for England's vital World Cup qualifying match in Rumania in October last year. It was the first time I had been included in the senior squad.

As there were no injuries with the big team England manager Ron Greenwood decided to play me in the Under-21 international on the eve of the main match. I was honoured to be named as captain.

The Rumanians gave us a 4-0 drubbing. It was a tough, physical match. As a team England were a disaster. I have played for Villa in U.E.F.A. Cup ties and made several other appearances for the Under-21's. But the rough-house tactics employed by the Rumanians were new to me.

I'm certain my experience in Ploesti will help me in the future. I know what to expect now if a team try to kick you off the park.

I didn't think my confidence was shattered by my bad show in Rumania or the team's lack-lustre performance. Yet my decline at Villa coincided with that England trip.

From winning my first call to the full England team I drifted off the international scene. That was a sickening blow.

A couple of years ago I was the only Villa man winning inter-national recognition. With the club chasing the League title last term there was a clamour of support for my team-mates,

Villa's GORDON COWANS looks back on an amazing season

Dennis Mortimer, Gary Shaw, Tony Morley, Kenny Swain and Peter Withe.

Yet I was left completely out of the reckoning by Mr Greenwood. I didn't even merit a call-up for the 'B' team.

The great factor that kept me plugging away through my bleak spell was the tremendous team spirit at Villa Park.

If I had to list the three main factors that took us to the First Division title I would place the players' fighting spirit as the main quality.

Every player was prepared to run and chase for his mates. The tremendous attitude carried us through on many occasions. At Everton, for instance, we didn't play particularly well. At one stage we looked like losing the game. But we all pulled together and finished 3-1 winners.

The second key reason for our success is the all-round ability in the side. From Jimmy Rimmer in goal to Tony Morley out on the left-wing there is a standard set for each player. Every Villa man knows he can do a good job as an individual and blend into the team set-up.

The third vital factor is the Villa men's will-to-win. You may think all players go out week in, week out determined to end up on the winning side. But when the going gets tough, it's pouring with rain and the pitch is a mud-bath some teams seem to ease up. Invariably they lose.

There is a great tradition at Aston Villa. The club is one of the oldest and most famous in the world. But too many of the great moments are in the past. Last term we were determined to make 1981 a year for the history books. And we certainly did that!

Like most players I have a lot of interests away from the game.

Many of the Villa lads are keen golfers and I enjoy the odd round. But my great release is watching greyhound racing.

I co-own four dogs with my father. And have another dog named Barcroft Baron in training.

Unlike horse racing, owning a winning greyhound will never make me rich. Forty pounds is a big pay-out at most tracks.

I suppose the one luxury I have bought from my football earnings is a rare Triumph TR 5 sports car. A couple of years ago I was named the best young player in England and won a Rover car. As I already owned a Ford Capri 3 litre it seemed pointless keeping the new motor. So I sold it and invested the money in the Triumph.

It is a red, open-topped car. Only 200 were made like mine so it is growing in value all the time. It does go very fast. I just wish my dogs could move at the same speed!

Talented team-mate, **TONY MORLEY** (*right*), in action against Manchester City's **TONY HENRY**.

TALES FROM TINY'S TRAVELS

YOU'VE probably heard jokes told about haggis which, says the dictionary, is " A Scottish dish made of the heart, lungs and liver of a sheep or calf, chopped up with suet, onions and oatmeal, seasoned and boiled in a sheep's stomach bag."

It's doubtful if you've ever heard it suggested this rather bizarre food mixture can give footballers special determination.

But until recently, there was an international team coach who seemed willing to believe it.

The story is told by Tom Wharton, the Scot who was a top international referee and is now a FIFA Referee Instructor.

Last season, during a 16-day tour of duty in China, Tom talked about football with the national coach.

The pair had agreed Chinese players were short of perseverance when the coach said it—" Maybe it's because we don't have haggis in this country."

It took the visitor from Scotland a minute or two to discover what lay behind this.

Said Tom Wharton—

" Apparently, during their tour in Britain, after the Chinese national team had lost 6-1 to Celtic, the Glasgow club's Chairman joked that the difference between the teams was that the Celtic players were brought up on haggis. That it gave them greater strength and determination."

And the Chinese gentlemen had taken the crack at face value . . .

There was a lot more fun on this trip " Big Tiny " made into some of football's least known corners.

He can still laugh about what happened at the last of a number of lectures he gave on the rules of football.

" I was approached very solemnly by a representative of China's Department of Physical Culture and Sport," he says. " He told me they had a big problem, and would I help them?

" When I said I'd be happy to he asked—Could I tell him the rules of CRICKET!

" It turned out that some visiting English VIP had presented the department with a full set of cricket gear—and they had no idea how to use it.

" I did my best to explain. Imagine—a Scotsman describing cricket to the Chinese!

" Anyhow, when I got home I sent them a book on the rules of the game.

Tom Wharton won't forget his time among the football folk of China. During 6000 miles of travel by air and rail, all his lectures were given simultaneous translation and seemed to go down in a big way.

He also saw the play-offs for the National Championships between the winners of the regional competitions made necessary in this vast land.

" The seniors played in Chungking, juniors in Hangchow. Using just one Stadium in each city, they put on three games a day with kick-offs at 11 o'clock in the forenoon and two and four in the afternoon.

" There were crowds of around 10,000. And, in accord with the country's low wages, they got the lot, in our money, for just 7½p."

GRAHAM RIX
Arsenal

85

FOOTBALL'S a FUNNY GAME!

They're so bad here they don't even have a popular end to the ground!

You wait till I get you home!

It's my chewing gum. It's lost its flavour!

The pitch is in good condit . . . !

Smith, from a pass by Brown!

IT'S HEADLINES ALL THE WAY

MANCHESTER UNITED are the biggest club in British football. Throughout my nine years at Old Trafford, United have continually hit the headlines.

Managers have been hired and fired. The club was relegated to the Second Division only to bounce straight back and emerge as a major force in English football.

And I have had my own fair share of bizarre events to prove life with Manchester United is never dull!

On my first day as a schoolboy trialist at Old Trafford I was beaten-up outside a fish and chip shop. Only 14 at the time, I was with five other lads from Northern Ireland who had been brought over by United's talent scout Bob Bishop. Hearing our Irish accents some older lads gave us a good hiding.

We were lucky Mr Bishop was carrying all our spending money in his wallet. If that had been stolen we would have been penniless.

Despite having a few bruises I quickly decided Manchester United was the club I wanted to join.

The manager who actually signed me was a quiet Irishman from Dublin called Frank O'Farrell.

I didn't have many dealings with Mr O'Farrell. He rarely went out on to the training ground with the players, spending most of the day behind his desk in the manager's office. Nobody seemed to know him.

When he was sacked, the irrepressible Tommy Docherty arrived on the scene. A man I will never forget.

I used to really look forward to training with the ' Doc.' On my way to the ground I would wonder what mad-cap trick the boss would pull that day. Who would be given a rollicking? Who would feel the sharp edge of Tommy's tongue?

I've seen the Doc send-off established international stars in training because they were not giving their all. He refused to let players become too satisfied with themselves.

Tommy Docherty also messed me around, giving me the most harrowing ten weeks of my career.

All the United apprentices were signed on professional terms on their seventeenth birthday. But my birthday came and went and still the boss made no effort to discuss my future.

When I was summoned to his office it was for a rollicking. I thought I was making good progress. My form had been praised by many coaches. Yet

Above —
FRANK O'FARRELL

Right —
TOMMY DOCHERTY

Docherty reckoned I was lazy and that my attitude was wrong.

To this day I still disagree with his opinion. But after two and a half months of sheer misery while I worried about my future with United I was signed as a professional. Even then the 'Doc' had to have a dig at me.

"You've not worked hard enough to win this contract. You need chasing too much," was his view.

Yet the same manager arranged for my parents to move out of Belfast into a club house in Manchester when he realised I was concerned about their safety in Northern Ireland. You just never knew how the 'Doc' would react.

After leading United out of the Second Division and to consecutive F.A. Cup finals,

however, Tommy was sacked. Dave Sexton replaced him.

Dave was a difficult man to get to know. He was just as shy and reserved as the 'Doc' had been brash and abrasive.

The club was heavily criticised when they sacked Mr Sexton at the end of last season.

Yet when I was sidelined with a muscle injury I sat in the main stand and realised how disillusioned the loyal United fans were with their team. We really struggled to entertain them. We'd lost the rhythm and style that made us so difficult to beat a couple of years earlier.

I never like to see anyone lose their job. Dave Sexton was an honest man. But the players never got close enough to him to understand his hopes and dreams for the club. For me it was not a blow when he left.

With United failing to get amongst the honours in recent years I have been particularly pleased with the way Northern Ireland's international standing has improved.

My Northern Ireland caps are some of my most precious possessions and yet I could have played for two other countries.

I was born in Hamilton, Ontario. So by birth I am a Canadian. My family moved back to Belfast when I was three.

My dad is Irish so that means I can genuinely wear the green jersey. But with a Scottish mother I do in fact qualify to play for Scotland.

By growing up in Belfast and playing for East Antrim Schoolboys and Northern Ireland Under-15's I feel I have proved myself a real Ulsterman. I have no doubts I am truly Irish—and proud of it.

IAN McCULLOCH
Notts County

89

I FELT LIKE QUITTING!

Middlesbrough's JIM PLATT tells why!

TWO things have happened to me over the past 12 months that fill me with pride and satisfaction.

First I was awarded a testimonial season by Middlesbrough to celebrate my 10 years at Ayresome Park. Then I was voted the North East's Player of the Year by the area's football writers.

To some that might not appear much. But for me they were events which gave me a very special satisfaction . . . because I could so easily not have been around to enjoy them!

Just over three years ago not only was my career with 'Boro in serious doubt, but my entire future as a professional footballer was in the balance.

Towards the end of season 77-78 and after years of being a ' regular ' in the side. I could see no future for myself with Middlesbrough.

Now, I'd have been the first to admit that over the previous couple of seasons my form had been inconsistent.

I'd have good games and then the not so good. It was this lack of consistency that saw me shuttled in and out of the side after being a 'fixture'.

But, even allowing for that, I'll never believe I was bad enough to warrant the kind of situation I found myself in. For not only was I out of the side, but I was also up for grabs at a transfer fee of just £25,000.

I thought that price was a 'snip' for a bloke who had played something in the order of £300 games. I reckoned some club . . . and a big one at that . . . would agree. But there were no takers.

Confidence was knocked right out of me. I could quite easily have 'dropped out' of football altogether.

Indeed, when the going was roughest, the thought of quitting and going home to a peaceful life in my native Ireland was never far from my thoughts.

Yet, in the end, it was one of those turns of fortune only football can throw up, that finally made me decide to stay in the game.

Despite being out in the cold at 'Boro, I was picked to play for Ireland in the home international against England at Wembley.

It turned out to be a very good evening for me. I enjoyed the game and played well. So well that even though my club manager John Neal went out the following day and signed Jim Stewart from Kilmarnock, all thoughts of jacking in the game were forgotten.

Of course, with Jim's arrival I knew the job of re-establishing myself at Ayresome Park was to be even more difficult. The boss clearly hadn't paid out a six figure fee to play Jim in the reserves.

But I suddenly realised that to quit would be taking the easy way out. For my own peace of mind I had to accept the 'challenge' and go flat out to prove I was no back number.

Not that it happened overnight. Indeed, I had to go through quite a few more months of deep depression before I got the chance to prove my worth in the first team again.

All the time, too, I accepted that if another club came in with an offer for my permanent transfer I'd have been ushered out the Teeside door. But even then there was irony in that situation. For it was only on the eve of my come-back for 'Boro that I got my first chance of a transfer.

After months when no interest was show in me, Blackburn Rovers wanted to buy me. I would have gone in a flash, but 'Boro said no.

Mind you, I doubt if the memory of that period in my life will ever completely desert me. Certainly it has taught me that you can never ever take anything for granted in this game.

To confirm the point I need only recall an experience of my own. Middlesbrough were playing Second Division Orient in the quarter-finals of the F.A. Cup. It was a tie we should have won easily to reach the semi-final stage for the first time in the club's history.

Instead we were held to a draw on our own pitch, taken to a replay in London and I was given a lot of stick over the goal that was to shatter our dreams.

I remember it well. The shot came in from about 30 yards. I was maybe down a shade early, but would still have been able to save the shot if the ball hadn't dipped in front of me and taken a bounce I just couldn't anticipate.

Of course, I felt bad about it. But now I simply look back and put it down to the harsh realities of being a goalkeeper.

Football is full of uncertainties. Things are either good or bad. There is no in-between.

The week before that Orient match, for example, we had drawn 0-0 with Manchester United at Old Trafford . . . and I saved a penalty. Fortunes can fluctuate so quickly . . .

Maybe that is why it has been said 'keepers have a daft streak in them. Certainly you've got to have a pretty thick skin to survive.

I'm just glad mine proved 'thick' enough when I was really put to the test!

JIM STEWART —
big-money buy, now back
in Scotland with Rangers.
He put the pressure on
for that first-team spot.

Peruvian side Los Terribles certainly lived up to their name in one particular match ... they were all sent off!

With their side leading 1-0 all eleven players promptly sat down on their goal line in protest at the ref's decision to award a penalty against them.

Firstly they were all shown the yellow card. And when they still refused to get up and continue, the referee pulled out his red card and it was an early bath for everyone.

Paolo Ammoniacci of Palermo must have set a record in a recent Italian League match.

He had been on the field only eleven seconds as a substitute when he was sent-off! Ammoniacci committed a brutal foul without ever touching the ball and was instantly dismissed.

Surely a world record.

You've heard of bonuses for winning but have you heard this one from Turkey ... £40 extra in their packets for losing 4-0!

That is what Orduspor, who were holding up the rest of the First Division, received in one partcular match. The explanation for this show of generosity was that the team had been expected to lose by at least 10-1.

The 22 players of Brazilian sides Babia and Ipiranga stood motionless as the National Anthem was played for the country's Independence Day.

Suddenly Babia's midfield man Edson started fidgeting and finally made a dash to the dressing-room as the Anthem played on.

Reason for his quick exit were ants! He had stood on a nest and had heroically remained at attention whilst they attacked his legs. But it became too much for him when the army marched on under his shorts!

★ ★ ★ ★ ★ ★ ★ ★ ★ ★ ★ ★ ★ ★ ★ ★ ★

Some of our referees may on occasions run into motoring hazards or bad weather conditions when they are driving up and down motorways to officiate at games.

But they have it cushy when you compare their problems with that of Brazilian ref Nacor Arouche. Having found his flight to Boa Vista would not arrive on time for him to get to the game he hired a taxi.

However, the cab broke down late at night in a thick jungle and an Indian tribe (Waimiris Atroaris) came along to investigate.

The ref was made to sit in the pouring rain as the tribe pulled his hair and looked into his mouth. Another car came along eventually and frightened them off.

Arouche learned later that the tribe had recently killed a traveller on that very same road!

★ ★ ★ ★ ★ ★ ★ ★ ★ ★

It was typical slapstick stuff straight out of a circus when Atlanta and Colo Colo met in a match in Chile.

Although it wasn't quite so amusing for Atlanta's Vasquez. He went down injured and two assistants had to race on with a stretcher.

Vasquez was gently placed on it then the stretcher bearers both walked off in opposite directions!

The unfortunate player was dumped back on the turf!

A Spanish Third Division player created a big mystery during one particular match. He had scored a goal and shortly after had to be helped off the pitch with very bad pains in his right foot.

The club doctor was mystified. He couldn't see any immediate reason for the terrible discomfort the player was obviously in.

Then when they arrived in the dressing room the player removed his boot and the offending pain was discovered ... there was a shoehorn inside!

How often have you heard the knowall next to you at a match say that he could do a better job than the referee?

Well, in Argentina one such loud-mouth was given the opportunity. The crowd had been somewhat noisy in their criticism of the poor man in black.

Finally he had enough, and walked off the pitch handing his whistle to one particularly abusive fan and told him to do the job himself!

The fan promptly did so, but was later bundled from the ground having awarded two unjustified penalties!

The match was rearranged.

JOHN WILE
West Bromwich Albion

93

LATE STARTER—
But I'll make up for that!

PAUL POWER of Manchester City — yet it could have easily been Paul Power of Washington Diplomats . . . or Sunderland . . . or New York Cosmos . . . or Wolverhampton Wanderers.

Because I'm the player City might have sold four times while I was attempting to establish myself in the Maine Road side.

Needless to say, I never moved. I didn't want to. All the offers were at the instigation of the would-be buyers and all but one were non-starters because City blocked the move.

New York's offer was the exception. That came at around the time Dennis Tueart moved there from Maine Road. They wanted me, too, but I didn't feel I was ready to move across the Atlantic so I turned them down.

Washington provided another opportunity for me to try my luck in the States. But City were in the middle of a good UEFA Cup run and as I was playing a part the manager at the time—Tony Book—said no.

Then Ian McFarlane, who left Maine Road to coach Sunderland a few years back, wanted to take me to Roker Park. He made City an offer but it was turned down.

My last chance to leave came when Malcolm Allison was in charge. He wanted to buy Steve Daley from Wolves. Their manager John Barnwell wanted me in part-exchange. Malcolm wouldn't hear of it, so he paid the full cash price for Steve.

Shortly after that, Mal handed me the skipper's job. For someone who hadn't any international honours it was probably the biggest personal achievement possible.

Vows Manchester City's skipper PAUL POWER

It's a marvellous feeling to lead out a team. After all, it isn't every player who can say they have captained a First Division side.

The honour means so much to me because I've been connected with City since I signed as an amateur at 17.

It was five years before I eventually turned pro. Doing a law degree at Leeds Polytechnic, I wanted to have that qualification just in case anything went wrong with my football career.

I did feel I'd missed out my early soccer apprenticeship. I wasn't as fit as I could have been for one thing. But I soon got over that. I believe that what I missed at the start of my career might well be tagged on at the end.

After all, my legs will have travelled those fewer miles, and that could be important. It's reckoned a midfield player like myself runs about seven or eight miles a game. As I didn't break into the first team until I was 22-23, I haven't run as far as most.

Look at Kevin Reeves, my Manchester City team-mate, for instance. Four years younger than me, he's made more League appearances. I just hope my late start will prolong my life as a First Division footballer.

Fitness is vital to my sort of game. My strong point is running ability. So it's important I don't fall from a peak level of fitness.

I am lucky I'm a left-sided player. There aren't too many of us around and it made it that bit easier to establish myself in the team.

I've been called a versatile player and that's true in that I can do a good job anywhere on the left flank.

I've alternated between left back and the left side of midfield during my career. I've not minded swopping around but it makes it difficult to call a position your own.

Since John Bond took over from Malcolm Allison as boss, I've been basically a midfielder. I'll fill in occasionally at full back if there's an emergency but the boss and I are convinced midfield is my best position.

Operating in the number three spot tends to show up deficiencies in my defensive abilities and my heading. On the left side of midfield I can give the side width and provide cover for the full back behind me.

A significant event in my career was when the club sold England winger Peter Barnes to West Bromwich Albion in 1979.

Peter played on the left wing at Maine Road. Unless I was playing at full back, it wasn't often there was room for both of us in the team.

We were really vying for the

PETER BARNES — his move was an important one for Paul Power.

same place and when City let Peter go I felt they were showing a lot of faith in me. I hoped it meant they thought I might be more valuable to the club in the long term. Peter's departure was one of the main reasons I eventually won a regular place in the side.

That was definitely the turning point. Up to then I'd been in out of the team. I didn't mind that, though. I realised my apprenticeship would last longer than most because of my late start.

I never despaired about making it in those early days. You only feel that if the club or the manager snubs you and I have to say that everyone at Maine Road has given me nothing but encouragement.

I've had my share of ups and downs since coming into the team, of course. There was the nightmare of a relegation battle before John Bond took over from Malcom Allison, for instance. That put all the players

under a lot of pressure at City.

The majority of the lads were all for Mal. But it was upsetting that his job was on the line. We went on to the field every week knowing we were playing to save that job.

John Bond arrived and removed that pressure. We climbed the table and had a couple of good cup runs.

Now I'm after my first medal. I haven't got much in my trophy cabinet—just a tankard for winning the Lancashire League Cup with City's reserves —so I'm desperate to start filling it up.

My most bitter dis-appointment was being beaten by Spurs in the '81 Cup Final. To have got so near and then lose out after a replay was hard to take.

This City side needs to win something to stamp its success. I believe we have the ability. It would be marvellous to be part of a team that lifts a trophy.

YOU CAN'T BEAT STRING!

Electronic crowd counters, Electric under-soil heating, giant pitch rollers—all part and parcel of football in the eighties. But some jobs still have to be done by old-fashioned methods. And for Crystal Palace groundsman John Plumber when it comes to marking the pitch—you can't beat string, almost half a mile of it in fact.

JOE GALLAGHER
Birmingham City

97

LUCKY, LUCKY ME

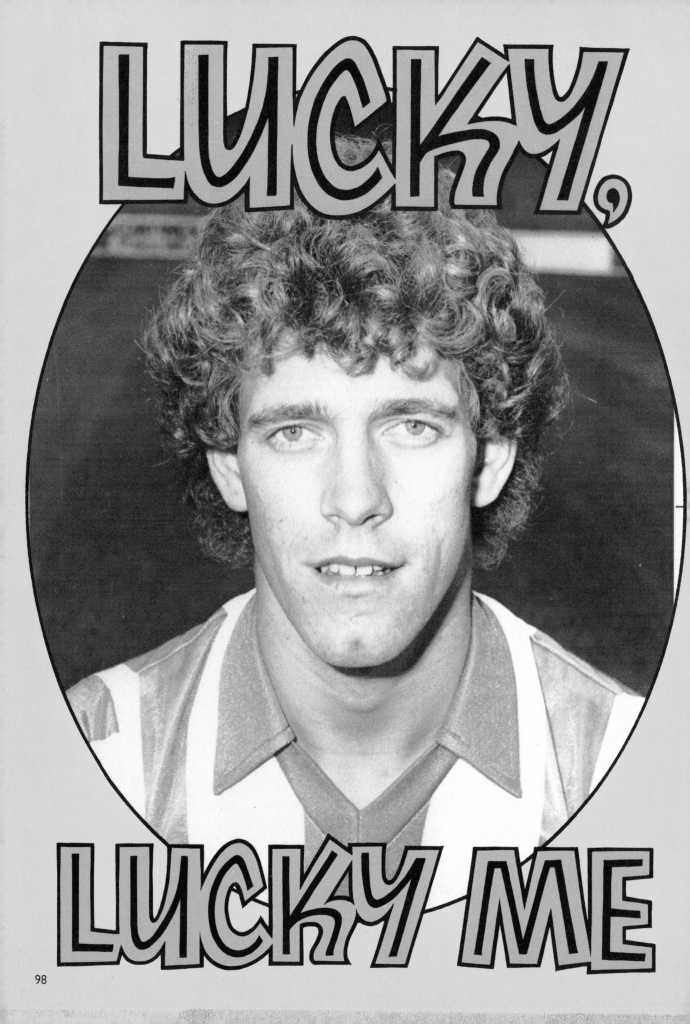

Sunderland's ROB HINDMARCH tells his story

LAST season I realised two boyhood ambitions. I played in the First Division with Sunderland, and became the youngest skipper in the club's history.

I was just 19 and it seemed no time at all since I'd been polishing players' boots as an apprentice with the club and, before that standing on the terraces as a spectator.

To suddenly be leading the team out at places like Old Trafford and White Hart Lane came as a complete surprise, albeit a pleasant one.

For, even though our then manager Ken Knighton had predicted only the season before that I would one day captain the side, I had no reason to believe it would happen so quickly.

To be honest I'd taken Ken's suggestion with a pinch of salt. At the time I'd played less than 20 first team matches . . . and my only real concern was to establish myself in the side.

At the beginning of last term, in fact, it appeared that I was going to have a bit of a wait to accomplish even that, let alone lead out the side.

Having helped the club back to the First Division I was 'dropped' after just four matches in the top-flight.

I was very disappointed about that . . . even though I knew I wasn't playing particularly well. I didn't enjoy missing out on the following 13 games either.

But, suddenly, things began to look up again. I was drafted back into the line-up and the boost of being made captain a few weeks later soon put all the dejection behind me.

I could only reflect that, but for the fact three other clubs had rejected me as a youngster, it all might never have happened.

As a fourteen-year-old I'd trained one night a week with arch-rivals Newcastle United . . . but they never attempted to sign me even on schoolboy forms.

Then I travelled down to Bolton to play a trial match . . . but was never asked back.

Spurs made up the trio who didn't want to know. I spent a week with them and felt terribly disappointed when they didn't make me any kind of offer at the end of it.

Disappointing at the time, yes. But all that was soon forgotten when Sunderland arrived on the scene. They didn't have to ask me twice to sign.

Nothing has happened since to make me think that I was wrong in throwing in my lot with the club which had always held a special meaning for me.

Not that I take anything for granted. In lots of ways I still consider I'm serving my apprenticeship at this game. I've got a fair bit to learn yet.

In fact, I don't think you can ever really learn enough in football. There is always something new waiting to be discovered just round the corner.

At 6 ft. 1 in. and thirteen and a half stone I've always been naturally good in the air. But I

know that there is still room for improvement in my game when it comes to 'on-the-deck' work. But that should come and I don't mind admitting my long term ambition is to play for England.

I have, in fact, already had experience of pulling on the white shirt. I played and captained the English youth side eight times in my early days at Roker Park.

It was a tremendous experience and gave me some insight to what it must be like representing your country at the very highest level.

People naturally ask me how I reacted to being skipper of the club last season . . . particularly over the closing weeks when we were fighting against relegation.

My answer is always the same . . . it didn't bother me in the slightest, even though I know it is a job that has affected players of much greater experience.

Even when we had to go to Anfield and beat Liverpool on the last day of the term to make sure of staying in the First Division I didn't feel under too much pressure or strain. Although I was pretty pleased when Stan Cummins got the vital goal!

Off the field I tend to be fairly quiet, but I've always been a bit of a talker on the pitch. I certainly don't have any qualms about making my feelings known.

For me, in fact, the real 'work' of being team captain is more concerned with off-field duties.

I'm the bloke with the responsibility of organising guest appearances by players at functions and presentations. There are also a multitude of other little things that take up your time, if you're captain.

Not that I mind that in the least. In fact, it is proof that I'm a very lucky man. That I've achieved a few things a lot of youngsters of my age can only dream about!

STAN CUMMINS—
he scored the vital goal.

Man. Utd's MARTIN BUCHAN (left) and Forest's TREVOR FRANCIS pull out all the stops in this mid-air duel.

JUMP TO IT

GEOFF PIKE
West Ham United

101

THEY'VE GOT BIG HEARTS AT THE DELL

SOUTHAMPTON SHOW HOW CLUBS CAN BE WINNERS OFF THE FIELD.

"**I**F we can do something to help a kid in a wheelchair we should do it."

The speaker is Lawrie McMenemy, and it's a pattern he put into practice at Southampton.

Southampton don't just work on the field at being a top football club. They always try to involve the local youngsters in the club.

No matter if they are kids who are kicking a ball about in the local park every day, or enthusiasts who because of some kind of disability can only watch.

None goes along with this more than Kevin Keegan. He tries to give us much of his time as possible to helping all youngsters—particularly the disabled.

Typical of the England skipper was the time he arranged for a group of spastic children to watch training at the Southampton ground. Then in addition he also arranged that they should have a free music centre.

One of Kevin's outside activities is tied up with Grundig, the German company. He asked his sponsors to supply the set free of charge to the handicapped kids.

Southampton organise regular opportunities for

Kevin Keegan with two admirers

LAWRIE McMENEMY

102

youngsters to watch their stars in training and it's not just the local youngsters.

Last season Southampton welcomed handicapped youngsters from as far afield as Doncaster and Grimsby.

The children are invited to the ground to watch the professionals train. They meet the players, are taken into the dressing rooms, and are generally entertained by the playing and training staff. All players get involved.

Typical of the attitude is the time a last-minute request came asking if the players could attend a party for spastic children. It came almost at the end of a training session when players were ready to go home for the afternoon.

It had to be a volunteer job, but eight first team players turned up. Two who did not go were under treatment for injury.

All of which adds to the Southampton reputation of being a 'homely' club. In football terms, they are from a small town with a ground that can never accommodate more than 26,000. They have to keep pace with teams from London, Liverpool, Manchester and Birmingham.

The way that they do it is to build up local contact, getting the club involved in all kinds of activities outside of football.

But on the big field, too, they can match the big clubs; winning the FA Cup in 1976; League Cup Finalists in 1979; playing in Europe, also producing home grown stars like Graham Baker and Steve Moran, or signing top names like Kevin Keegan, Charlie George, Dave Watson, Alan Ball, and Chris Nicholl.

All big names—and all playing their part in making a club like Southampton very much part of the local scene.

Not just for the fans who can get on the terraces every week, but the youngsters who are handicapped and can't be there to cheer on their team.

It's a pattern laid down by Lawrie McMenemy.

"I feel that we should give something to handicapped children," he said at the start of it all. It's a lesson for all clubs.

Southampton players meet the fans—bringing happy smiles from the youngsters.

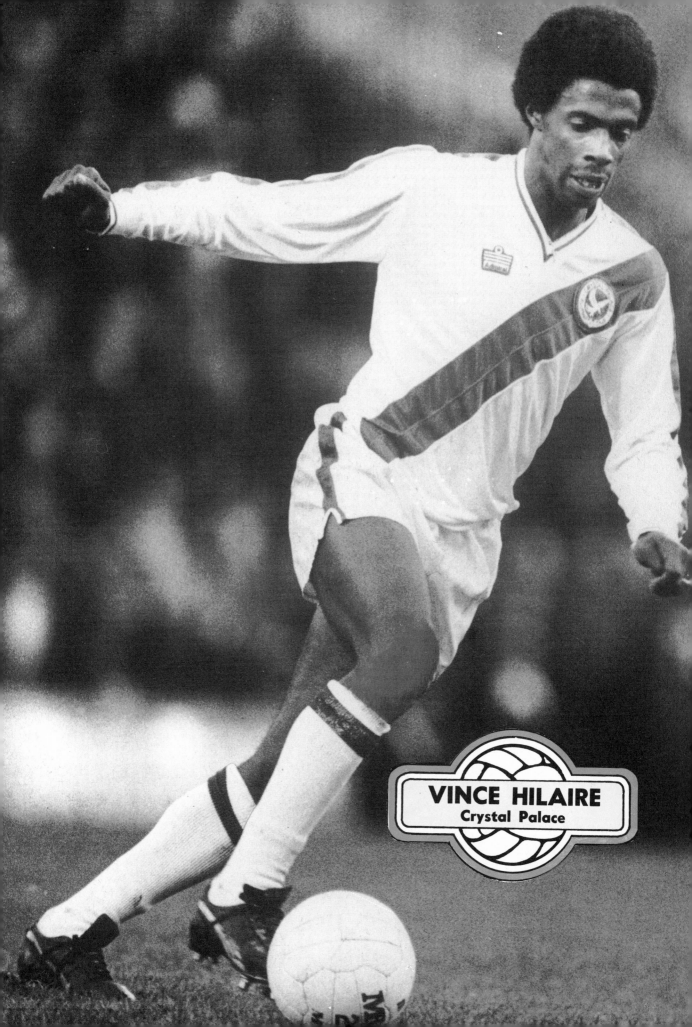

VINCE HILAIRE
Crystal Palace

NO HOLDS BARRED!

They're not the biggest players in the game—but when it comes to determination and will-to-win, they don't come any more whole-hearted than Liverpool's SAMMY LEE and Leeds BRIAN FLYNN. Action like this is typical of these two battlers.

J. Rico Perez

San Mames

Santiago Bernabeu

R.C.D. Espanol

Riazor

Nuevo Estadio

El Molinon

Carlos Tartiere

Vincente Calderon

R. Sanchez Pizjuan

La Rosaleda

SPAIN and Brazil came to Wembley near the end of last season and beat England. Spain are automatic World Cup qualifiers as the home country. Brazil were the first side to win their qualifying section.

Both showed that when the World Cup kicks off in Spain in 1982, they will be teams to reckon with.

Add to that Argentina as the holders and the pattern is set for the 1982 World Cup.

A battle between Europe and South American but with a vital difference from previous tournaments.

Both the Argentine and Brazil have played in Europe as part of their build-up. Learning all about European conditions and European styles.

They aim to "marry" the traditional ball-playing style of the South Americans with the aggressive tackling of the European sides. On the evidence so far, the South American teams have learned to play in Europe.

When European national teams went to Uruguay for a competition for former World Cup winners they were surprised that all the South American countries had added ball winning to their ball playing skills.

In the last two European World Cup Finals, South American countries fared none too well. In 1966, Brazil failed to get beyond their opening group. Argentina were beaten by England in the quarter-finals. No South American team reached the semi-final stage.

Much the same happened in West Germany in 1974 when Brazil could do no better than finish forth, behind West Germany, Holland and Poland.

Traditionally the host country does well in the World Cup Finals. Spain believe that in 1982 they can win the World Cup for the first time. Playing in their South American style, and having the experience of playing against the hard tackling European sides—they combine the two qualities that are seen as being a must for World Cup success.

For the first time there will be twenty-four countries playing in Spain, instead of the sixteen teams as in previous competitions.

The matches will be spread over fourteen centres, the main ones being the Bernabeu Stadium in Madrid, and the Nou Camp Stadium in Barcelona.

Then add names like Valencia, Elche, Alicante, Zaragoza, Bilbao, Valladolid, Curuna, Vigo, Giljon, Malaga, Seville and Oviedo.

It should be a well organised World Cup. Spain sent observers to study the organisation in the Argentine. And they know all about making arrangements for a mass of visitors.

In a normal summer, Spain accommodates thirty-nine million holiday-makers. There are over 7,000 hotels, an amazing half million beds. They do not expect any problems

with grounds or accommodation.

Thirty million pounds was the figure given for ground improvements. To be paid for with the help of a National Lottery.

Even before the majority of the world had finalised the twenty-four qualifiers, the money had been found—with some to spare.

There was a turnover of 22 million pounds during the World Cup in the Argentine. This is expected to be beaten in Spain.

The world TV rights have been sold for £10½ million, Advertising on grounds adds another £10 million; there are special stamps, coins and mascots that are expected to bring in £8 million.

For almost the first time the country staging the World Cup Finals will show a profit. Mainly because the Spanish grounds, apart from minor improvements, are already available and fit to stage the world's top football tournament.

In addition there is the problem of looking after the needs of the world media. 10,900 seats will be put at the disposal of the Press. There will be 3,840 telephones to carry up-to-the minute news all over

Balaidos

Benito Villamarin

Luis Casanova

Nou Camp

La Romareda

the world. Plus 1,875 seats for radio and television commentators, and 3,750 TV sets to keep everyone informed. There will be 1,160 photographers with Press rooms, radio boxes and TV points.

All the organisation is available to make the Spanish World Cup an occasion for the fans from Europe who know all about the Spanish ability to accommodate tourists. But no matter the organisation the success of any World Cup is still down to the quality of football.

And who better to talk about that than Pele, perhaps the best known World Cup player of all time.

As a seventeen-year-old, he was in the Brazilian team that won the World Cup in Sweden in 1958. Four years later in Chile another winners' medal came his way.

In England in 1966, Brazil failed to win their qualifying section after Pele was brutally fouled in two games, but in 1970 at the age of 29, Pele lead Brazil in Mexico to their third World Cup win.

"Playing in the World Cup in Europe is so different to playing in the World Cup in South America," he said when he was on a European tour at the close of last season.

"The conditions are different. The style of play is harder. I think that Brazil, and the other South American teams, have discovered this. They will have changed their style to fit in with the tougher European conditions.

"Winning in the World Cup is a must for every Brazilian player," says Pele.

"In Spain the conditions and the crowd atmosphere will be very similar to playing in South America.

"That should suit the Latin temperament.

"Perhaps a South American team can follow Brazil and win again in Europe."

That's a tip from the top. But whatever happens it's bound to be a football fiesta in Spain next summer.

ESPAÑA 82

GIJON
OVIEDO
BILBAO
LA CORUNA
VIGO
ZARAGOZA
BARCELONA
VALLADOLID
MADRID
VALENCIA
ALICANTE
SEVILLA
ELCHE
MALAGA

Nuevo Estadio

MICK MILLS
Ipswich Town

NOEL BROTHERSTON
Blackburn Rovers

109

WOLVES

MOLINEUX, Wolverhampton Wanderers' ground, has been reshaped into one of the most modern grounds in England.

But not even an army of workmen with bulldozers will be able to demolish the memories conjured up by the famous gold and black Wolves.

Down the years they have been at the forefront of British football. It is a history packed with incident and drama.

Started by a group of schoolboys in 1877 they have become one of the most famous and respected clubs in the land.

The lads played under the name of their school—St Luke's, Blackenhall at their ground, Goldthorn Hill. After moving to Dudley Road in 1884 the club amalgamated with another team called the Wanderers three years later.

It was then they adopted their present title of Wolverhampton Wanderers. And in 1888 they became one of the founder members of the Football League.

In their very first season they finished third and in front of a record crowd of 22,000 at the Oval they lost 3-0 to Preston, the 'Invincibles', in the FA Cup Final.

A FAMOUS CLUB LOOKING TO THE FUTURE

In 1893, however, they finally won the first of their four FA Cups. But it was a final laced with controversy. A week earlier Everton, their opponents in the Cup, fielded a team of reserves in a league match against Wolves and beat them 4-2.

Naturally the Liverpudlians were hot favourites to land the trophy. But at Fallowfield, Manchester, the Wanderers won 1-0.

The ground was quite simply not suitable to house a tie as big as this. Crowds spilled over fences and were even sitting on the pitch. But the result stood despite a strong protest from the losers.

Despite a Cup Final defeat from Sheffield Wednesday in 1896 and a surprise victory over Newcastle in 1908, in between they had suffered relegation from the First Division and there was a lull for thirteen years.

They reawoke in 1921 to reach their fifth Cup Final only to lose to Spurs. Two years later they found themselves relegated to the Third Division.

In 1932 they regained their Division One status and soon the arrival as manager of Major Frank Buckley brought a transformation that put Wolverhampton Wanderers back amongst the sporting headlines.

The Major was never one to miss a chance to get the Wolves in print. He introduced psychology into football when he sent a number of his players in 1939 to a local psychologist to discuss their form!

Buckley had already created an even bigger footballing sensation by putting the Molineux players on a course of injections!

Huge headlines proclaimed that Wolves players were having 'monkey gland' treatment. But, in truth the injections weren't anything more than immunization against the common cold!

Nonetheless, that season Wanderers went to their very first Wembley final.

On paper Wolves only had to arrive at the ground to land the trophy against First Division strugglers Portsmouth.

But in practice it didn't work out. Wolves suffered a huge attack of nerves and went down by 4-1. Portsmouth skipper Jimmy Guthrie related afterwards he told his players that Wanderers were nervous because an autograph book Wolves signed before the game went into the Portsmouth dressing room and the signatures of the Wolves' players were spidery and shaky!

Despite that setback Buckley's young outfit, who had been title runners-up two year running, were ready to blossom fully. But the Second World War stopped their march.

Then after the war Wolves, under new management firstly with Ted Vizard and then Stan Cullis, became a powerful force in the forties and fifties.

Between 1947 and 1961 they won the League Championship three times, were runners-up three times and were third on four occassions.

In 1960 they almost became the first club in modern times to achieve the double. They won the FA Cup but failed to land a third successive title by a single point.

Whilst they were picking up the honours on home soil in the fifties they also blazed a trail in Europe, arranging friendlies against the likes of Honved, Real Madrid and Spartak of Russia.

It was a glorious era that also boasted the England skipper Billy Wright at Molineux. While wearing the gold and black he played 105 times for his country.

The run of success faded in the sixties and seventies and Second Division promotion battles and two League Cup final victories in 1974 and '80 were the only notable achievements.

But Wolverhampton Wanderers have still kept ahead of the rest of football off the field. In 1980 they broke the £1½ million barrier in the transfer market when manager John Barnwell purchased Andy Gray from Aston Villa. Then they started work on the ground, building a new £2½ million cantilever stand with even more developments to follow.

On and off the field the gold and black of Wolverhampton Wanderers still flies proudly.

Top — FRANK BUCKLEY
Centre — STAN CULLIS
Bottom — JOHN BARNWELL
Left — BILLY WRIGHT and the cup-winning Wolves

PAT BYRNE
Leicester City

112

IT HAPPENED LAST SEASON

1. Ipswich Town players scooped the PFA Player of the Year awards. Can you name the three top men and the order in which they finished?

2. One side had the unusual honour of being relegated with a positive goal difference. Who were they?

3. Which League side played the most FA Cup matches in 1980-81?

4. Who was the Football League's leading scorer in domestic competitions?

5. A last minute penalty was missed in the Scottish Cup Final. Who took it—and who saved it?

6. Which manager steered a side to eventual promotion, but ended the season with a relegated outfit?

7. He began the season as a Third Division manager and ended it playing in the First. Can you name him?

8. He played only one League Cup match all season but won a medal. Who was he?

9. Which was the first club to win promotion and the first to be relegated?

10. In Aston Villa's League Championship team how many players were ever-presents?

11. Name the English clubs who played in European competitions last season.

12. Who was picked as player of the year by Scotland's sports writers?

13. Which player played the most competitive matches last term?

14. Two Scottish players scored two hat-tricks in Europe for English clubs. Can you name the players and clubs?

15. Two First Division 'keepers were given the captaincy. One for his club, the other for his country. Names and teams, please.

Answers on page 125.

GEORGE McCLUSKEY
Celtic

115

DRAMA AT

A Cup Final goal is always a dramatic moment, and none more so than this one in the 1981 Wembley final, Spurs' equaliser against Manchester City.

GLENN HODDLE fires a free kick at the City goal.

PUZZLE ANSWERS

WORLD CUP PLAYERS

1—Italy	6—Italy
2—West Germany	7—West Germany
3—Brazil	8—Italy
4—Spain	9—Poland
5—Holland	10—Austria

TEN-YEAR QUIZ

1972—Glasgow Rangers.	1977—Wolves
1973—Liverpool.	1978—Nottingham Forest
1974—West Germany.	1979—Shrewsbury Town.
1975—Bayern Munich.	1980—Aberdeen.
1976—Liverpool.	1981—Southend United.

CROSSWORD

WEMBLEY
—THE STEP-BY-STEP BUILD UP TO A VITAL GOAL

The ball flies through the "wall" and heads straight for City's TOMMY HUTCHISON.

Joy for Spurs—despair for City. The ball ricochets off Hutchison into the City net.

ODD Spots

1—Coventry City.
2—They are the only club with a J in their name.
3—(a) Derby Country, (b) Wrexham, (c) Kilmarnock.
4—They are both nick-named "Dons."

FACE NAME
Dalglish

GUESS WHO
Danny Blanchflower.

GOALKEEPERS IN HIDING

S	Y	V	R	H	T	Y	L	B	A	R	S
A	P	E	N	O	T	L	I	H	S	E	E
T	T	A	L	P	U	O	T	E	K	P	K
J	E	N	N	I	N	G	S	A	N	O	R
D	O	O	W	Y	A	D	H	N	U	O	A
N	E	D	D	O	G	B	R	O	T	C	P

Rough · Shilton · Jennings · Bailey · Platt · Cooper · Day · Tunks · Godden · Parkes · Wood · Blyth

117

ALL CHANGE FOR CHARLTON

A strange sight for any fan—it's Bobby Charlton wearing the dark blue of Scotland. In a testimonial game Bobby turned out for a Scotland side against an England team. And he scored for the Dark Blues!

BRENDAN O'CALLAGHAN
Stoke City

THE RISE AND RISE OF SWANSEA CITY

Success Story That Made History

SWANSEA CITY set a Football League record by rising from the Fourth Division to the First in the space of four hectic seasons.

Now the Welsh club is enjoying life at the top for the very first time—using the same kind of careful planning that won them three promotions to ensure they stay with the elite. Plus a place in the European Cup Winners' Cup this season.

Yet all that success started by chance—the day John Toshack agreed to do some promotional work in Swansea while he was still a Liverpool player.

In March 1978, as Liverpool approached the quarter-finals of the European Cup, John Toshack was out of the first team set-up.

At the same time Swansea City were looking for an inspirational manager to clinch promotion from the Fourth Division.

Swansea Chairman Malcolm Struel heard that Toshack was visiting town and arranged a meeting on the spur of the moment.

Within days John Toshack was Swansea's new player-manager—and the club has never looked back since.

In each of their three promotion campaigns they have gone into the final match of the season needing a win to make sure.

They beat Halifax 2-0 to win promotion from Division IV. Beat Chesterfield 2-1—after being 1-0 down—to scrape into a promotion place from Division III. And last season went to Preston North End in the last match to win 3-1 and clinch a place in the First Division.

That demonstrates there's no lack of strong nerves at Vetch Field. Perhaps one of the qualities Toshack took with him from Liverpool.

From his early days with Swansea Toshack decided he would base his managerial style on the successful methods employed at Anfield by men like Bill Shankly and Bob Paisley.

He was a frequent Liverpool visitor, first learning from the backroom men and then picking up some of their most experienced players, like Ian Callaghan and Tommy Smith, on bargain transfers.

Toshack occasionally took his whole squad to Anfield to absorb the atmosphere and learn from the masters.

Callaghan and Smith became key men in the Swansea side, and Toshack added others such as Phil Boersma and Alan Waddle who were Anfield trained.

Swansea even began to be known as 'Liverpool reserves', but that didn't do justice to home bred stars like Robbie James, Jeremy Charles and Alan Curtis—who was sold to Leeds and then bought back—and signings like David Giles, Leighton Phillips and Leighton James.

Welsh international heroes such as Phillips, Leighton James, John Mahoney and Curtis, have re-vitalised their careers with Swansea.

It was also a shrewd investment in experience. The quality that is probably more vital than any other when it comes to winning promotion from the Second Division.

In his quiet way manager Toshack has joined the big spenders. In four seasons he has splashed out over £1 million.

Goalkeeper Dave Stewart (WBA) £55,000, full-back Dzemal Hadziabdic (Velez Mostar in Yugoslavia), £160,000, Tommy Craig (Aston Villa) £150,000, John Mahoney (Middlesbrough) £100,000, David Giles (Wrexham) £70,000, Leighton James (Burnley) £130,000, Dave Rushbury (Sheffield Wednesday) £60,000, Brian Attley (Cardiff) £20,000, Alan Curtis (Leeds) £175,000 being the main deals.

The sale of Curtis to Leeds for £400,000 helped to balance the books, but basically Swansea have treated the transfer fees as an investment in the future of the club.

JOHN TOSHACK—
urging his team on to victory.

TOMMY CRAIG — in a celebration mood.

They will carry on spending to improve the standard of the squad. Having reached the First Division Swansea will aim to win it as soon as possible.

"We don't use the word 'consolidation'." says Chairman Malcolm Struel. "Whatever competition you are in you must strive to win it. Consolidation is another word for stagnation in my book."

Brave words from the man who took over the helm at Vetch Field when the club was £¼ million in the red, about to apply for re-election to the Fourth Division, with gates at an all-time low of 2,000—and the creditors banging on the door.

It was an unpromising situation to present to the Football League AGM—a 'bed of nails' is how Chairman Struel described it. At the League meeting Struel made a remarkable prophecy.

"Give us time, and we can get to the First Division," he told the delegates who were about to vote on Swansea's future.

There was plenty of mirth at that remark—but the clubs voted Swansea back in.

At one time the club was 24 hours away from being wound up. But the Chairman sold the ground back to the local council to stave off some pressing debts, and provide breathing space.

Next move was to re-organise the commercial department. From a turn-over of only £15,000 in 1974, Swansea are now looking for an annual income of £250,000 from their lotteries, advertising, programmes, souvenirs and other schemes.

But the master stroke was still the appointment of John Toshack—thanks to that chance visit to Swansea. His signing acted as an inspiration to players and supporters alike.

"When I went into management I was determined to be a success." says Toshack.

"I have deliberately done things the Liverpool way because their methods are proven. They certainly haven't done badly by them!

"You can't stand still in this game. You must always look ahead and keep trying to improve."

That attitude is strong evidence of the determination of everyone involved with Swansea City to keep moving forward, to acquire the best players available—and to maintain the Liverpool connection.

It's a formula that has proved a winner for Swansea City. Fourth Division to First inside four years. And now the target is the Championship.

The ups and downs of football. NOBBY STILES, manager of relegated Preston, congratulates JOHN TOSHACK.

ALAN CURTIS
Swansea City

122

STEVE MORAN
Southampton

YOUR PICTURE GUIDE

QUIZ ANSWERS from page 113

1. 1st John Wark, 2nd Frans Thijssen, 3rd Paul Mariner.
2. Sheffield United.
3. Wolverhampton Wanderers.
4. Tony Kellow (Exeter City) 32 goals.
5. Hamish McAlpine (Dundee United) saved from Ian Redford (Rangers).
6. Dario Gradi. Moved from Wimbledon, who were eventually promoted to Crystal Palace who were relegated.
7. Alan Ball. Blackpool player/manager to Southampton.
8. Ian Rush (Liverpool).
9. Southend and Crystal Palace respectively.
10. Seven players were ever present. Rimmer, Swain, McNaught, Mortimer, Bremner, Cowans and Morley.
11. Liverpool, Nottingham Forest (European Cup). West Ham (Cup Winners Cup). Ipswich, Manchester United and Wolves (UEFA Cup).
12. Alan Rough (Partick Thistle).
13. Russell Osman (Ipswich Town).
14. Graeme Souness (Liverpool) and John Wark (Ipswich).
15. Mark Wallington for Leicester City. Ray Clemence (Liverpool) for England.

Printed and Published in Great Britain by D. C. THOMSON & CO., LTD., 185 Fleet Street, London EC4A 2HS. © D. C. THOMSON & CO., LTD., 1981.
ISBN 0 85116 221 5